Popular Culture and New Media

Popular Culture and New Media

The Politics of Circulation

David Beer
University of York, UK

First published 2013 by
PALGRAVE MACMILLAN

Palgrave Macmillan in the UK is an imprint of Macmillan Publishers Limited, registered in England, company number 785998, of Houndmills, Basingstoke, Hampshire RG21 6XS.

Palgrave Macmillan in the US is a division of St Martin's Press LLC, 175 Fifth Avenue, New York, NY 10010.

Palgrave Macmillan is the global academic imprint of the above companies and has companies and representatives throughout the world.

Palgrave® and Macmillan® are registered trademarks in the United States, the United Kingdom, Europe and other countries.

ISBN 978–1–137–27004–7

This book is printed on paper suitable for recycling and made from fully managed and sustained forest sources. Logging, pulping and manufacturing processes are expected to conform to the environmental regulations of the country of origin.

A catalogue record for this book is available from the British Library.

A catalog record for this book is available from the Library of Congress.

For Erika

Contents

Acknowledgements

As musicians often used to write in the notes on record sleeves, the people I want to thank know who they are. I'd most like to thank Martha and Erika (to whom this book is dedicated) as well as Bill, Barbara and Amanda and the rest of my family. I'd also like to thank my various collaborators; Nick Gane and Roger Burrows have been particularly helpful in the various stages of research that have culminated in this book. But more broadly I have enjoyed writing and discussing ideas with lots of people over the last ten years of research. My thanks also go to the publishers of this book. Finally, I'd like to thank and remember my friend and colleague Mike Hardey, who sadly died at around the time I started writing this book.

1

Introduction: The Intersections of Popular Culture and New Media

Some very ordinary but nonetheless very important things happen as popular culture interweaves with new media forms. It is here, in these remediations, that we find some of the defining experiences of contemporary everyday life. These are mainstream experiences that raise important questions about the organisation, relations and ordering of culture. Millions of people on a global scale are engaging with culture via these new media forms as they enchant, distract, entertain, reveal and occupy. Indeed, the intersection of popular culture and new media is at the heart of many of the big social and cultural issues that we face today. From issues of freedom of speech and the right to privacy, through to the massive revenues of the so-called digital economy, to forms of mass communication, expression and moralising, and on to questions about the nature of contemporary social connections and senses of difference.

The intersections of popular culture and new media have become central in shaping our everyday lives and in ordering our routine experiences. In many ways it has now become almost impossible to think of popular culture outside of its new media infrastructures. Similarly, when thinking of new media, we should be thinking of the popular forms of culture that are a central part of their use and incorporation into everyday practice. Yet, despite their prominence and interconnectivity, we often think of them as disconnected entities. In this book I attempt to situate popular culture, and even culture more generally, within the new media context. It is suggested that our understanding of both is improved where we think of these apparently separate spheres together. Hence, this is a book about popular

1

culture *in* new media. The story is told through a focus upon the new media infrastructures that afford what I describe here as *the circulations of popular culture*. The book elaborates these circulations by thinking across different scales or dimensions within the assemblage of popular culture and new media, starting with the way we conceptualise these infrastructures and objects and working through to the specifics of archives, algorithms, data play and the body. The book looks at a series of questions to understand these relations and data circulations. I ask how data accumulate as a result of the changing nature of objects and infrastructures. I then use the concept of archiving to ask how these accumulating data are ordered and organised. I ask how these accumulated data are made visible or utilised by automated algorithmic systems, and how these data are appropriated into practice through various types of play. And I then ask how the body can be placed into these data circulations to understand their corporeal affects. The hope is that this focus will reveal the nature of popular culture and new media today and will illustrate the importance of thinking about them together. Also, rather than starting with any crude definitions of popular culture or new media, the book is used to describe and elaborate the forms they take as they materially enmesh in different ways across the broader social and cultural context and within the instantiations of everyday life. The book then is concerned with how popular culture and new media intersect in the context of day-to-day life and in the circulations and infrastructures that underpin it. By bringing to the fore the material dimensions of everyday life, embodied in these infrastructures and data circulations, we are able to see how culture and media combine and fold into ordinary routine life.

As this indicates, this is a book about the way in which new media are transforming popular culture. More specifically, this book focuses upon the different ways that digital data circulate through popular culture; it is here that we can locate an underlying politics of circulation. It begins by looking at the *infrastructures* and *objects* that allow digital data to be generated through routine engagements with popular culture. It then uses this as a foundation for exploring the different flows, blockages and manipulations of these data through an examination of the part that *archives*, *algorithms*, *data play* and *the body* perform in such flows. As this suggests, the book moves from the pathways of data circulation to look at how these circulations operate, shift and reshape culture itself. This then is to focus upon what Adrian Mackenzie (2005) has called the 'performativity of circulation' and to locate it within popular culture. It is also to evoke Lee and LiPuma's (2002) notion of 'cultures of circulation'. Lee and LiPuma explore how circulation is a concept that might be explored in order to understand contemporary globalised culture from an economic perspective. They suggest that:

> If circulation is to serve as a useful analytical construct for cultural analysis, it must be conceived as more than simply the movement of people, ideas, and commodities from one culture to another. Instead, recent work indicates that circulation is a cultural process with its own forms of abstraction, evaluation, and constraint, which are created by the interactions between specific types of circulating forms and the interpretative communities built around them. It is in these structures that we identify cultures of circulation.
>
> (Lee and LiPuma, 2002: 192)

Lee and LiPuma describe in some detail the various conceptual origins of this position. But what I try to do in this book is to explore this notion of circulation as it materialises or becomes instantiated in the mediation of popular culture. At this point the circulations take on a very specific form; here the circulations I am referring to are circulations of data. This is something I have referred to elsewhere as the 'social life of data' (Beer and Burrows, 2013). The book attempts to update our understandings of contemporary culture by unpicking its everyday materiality in a changing socio-technological context. It uses various resources and materials to uncover the systems and flows that are now coming to shape and constitute what popular culture is, how it is organised, how it is disseminated and how tastes are formed.

The intention of this book then is to expand the analytical scope of studies of culture by adding a more material dimension to the debates, and by beginning to reveal how changing technological infrastructures require us to rethink and rework many of the assumptions we have about the organisation and relations of popular culture. Take, for example, the issue of cultural tastes and preferences. Cultural tastes are often understood to be a product of our social position, our friendship groups or taste communities, the subculture we might associate with and so on. We have little understanding though of how software algorithms are coming to shape cultural taste as they make recommendations to us and in so doing transform our cultural encounters (see Chapter 4 in particular). This book explores a number of such examples of recombinant cultural formations and how these data flows are channelled, directed, blocked and stimulated. Underpinning these explorations is the central argument that emergent circulations of data have now come to shape what popular culture is and how it is experienced. Data in various forms, often as metrics and other types of numeric measures (Burrows, 2012), now accumulate and feed back into the production, dissemination and consumption of culture in innumerable and often unseen ways. The book begins by showing how these digital by-product data are generated, it then moves towards an understanding of how these by-product data circulate back into culture with multifarious affects. I argue that these complex data circulations have become central to the forms that popular culture now takes, I also argue that popular culture is now defined by its recursive data flows and that this requires some careful consideration in order for us to fully understand what this means for culture more generally. My central aim will be to make clear that the study of contemporary culture requires an understanding of these circulations, the folding back of data into culture and the material infrastructures that make them possible.

A note on writing a book about new media and popular culture

Before starting though, I'd like first to highlight a problem that has shaped the direction and approach that this book takes. We know that writing a book is a relatively slow process, although I'm sure, like many aspects of our social and cultural lives, it has been the site of apparent speed-up (Gane, 2006; Tomlinson, 2007). This book is an old media format that moves somewhat slower than the types of media format and infrastructures that I am attempting to write about. This is not a problem in itself, it is likely to be helpful to balance rapid responses with slower more considered accounts of the phenomena under consideration (Atkinson and Beer, 2010). However, this is something that needs to be considered in the design and formulation of a book such as this. As you will no doubt have gathered, and as I discuss in far more detail in the following chapters, this is a book that in very general terms deals with the interfacing of popular culture and emergent or new media forms. The problem concerning the speed of publishing infrastructures is exacerbated in the case of this particular topic (Beer and Burrows, 2007). Popular culture and new media, particularly when in tandem, move together quite rapidly, plus they are defined by ephemerality, fragmentation and splintering. They are in flux, they are protean and mobile, transient and changeable, chaotic and ephemeral.

So, in short, the question is simply this, how can we productively write a book about popular culture and new media? This is a problem I've discussed and encountered in various forms in earlier pieces (Beer and Burrows, 2007; Beer, 2009a; Gane and Beer, 2008). The problem is one of keeping-up. Once something that is so changeable is written about then we might wonder what use or value is the text. We might argue that it is a historical document of that moment. This is fine, but it is only one moment, it is non-transferable, it is locked and immobile. There will undoubtedly be some of those moments in this book, moments when I will move towards a material application of the ideas that will induce a descriptive snapshot of something that is happening whilst the book is being written but which is unlikely to still exist when you, hopefully, read it.

In this context, it is pertinent to consider how it is possible to put together a book that might still be of potential use across temporal, spatial and cultural boundaries. How can a book about popular culture and new media be of use to readers whenever or wherever it is that they encounter it? How can a book speak to the reader across the transformations that might be occurring? How can the book still be of some analytical use if the culture it encounters has the potential to change so radically? Of course it is impossible to completely resolve these questions. Yet there seems greater necessity in a book, than in a journal article, to keep these questions at the forefront of how the piece is written. In response, in this particular text, I have chosen to place the balance of the work towards a conceptual engagement with the issues. There remain some specific details and descriptions in the book: these are needed to ground the work in the materiality of the culture it attempts to engage with. These details are used though to open up a range of conceptual questions. Even where their cultural experiences may vary from those offered in these descriptions, it is hoped that the reader will find some mileage in the conceptual ideas that emerge from these moments of empirical engagement and the conceptual connections and emergences that they provoke. I hope that you will forgive any moments that seem out-of-date or culturally irrelevant at the time of reading, and I hope still further that you will find something in the conceptual ideas to disagree with or to apply to whatever it is that is happening when this text is being read. I would also add that there is a pressing need more generally for a renewed conceptual engagement with culture that updates and re-energises older concepts and that furnishes these with a creative new conceptual vocabulary (Gane and Beer, 2008).

Of course, at the heart of my concerns are the broader problems that might be associated with the endless pursuit of the 'new' (see Savage, 2009a) that has come to define much of the social sciences. Nowhere is this more acute, perhaps unsurprisingly, than in work on new media. Here it is expected that work aims to uncover what is happening, what are the new or fresh phenomena or how the world is changing in fundamental ways. Often this is told through the microcosm of specific web sites or new devices. I closed my previous co-authored book (Beer and Gane, 2008) by outlining some of the problems with the category of 'new media'. First, much of the new media we discuss is often not all that new – such as the internet, mobile phones and laptops. This is not really a significant problem, continuity is important, but it just makes the prefix 'new' seem a bit strange, analytically awkward or even a little confusing. And, second, and closely related to this first point, is what the very concept of 'new media' forces the person analysing it to do. The problem is that it ties us into always looking for what is new at the expense of continuity, it forces us to ignore stable and established media, even those that have perhaps not received any critical or analytical attention, and to always be looking for the next development. This is the trap of newness that fits with the problems Savage (2009a) has outlined with regards to the drive to always be looking for the new and for change, rather than balancing this with a more considered and contextual outlook. I try to keep these in mind in this book and to think about continuity as well as change, to think about the historical development and fixity of the materialities of culture, as well as their reshaping, and to think contextually about media and culture as being a part of much broader social processes and forces. I also try to think of overarching and longer-term developments, those general trends that might be observed, rather than small changes to individual media in isolation.

With these issues in mind, the terms 'new media' and 'popular culture' become terms of convenience here that help to situate the work and to provide an indexical backdrop, but they are not limiting or defining in the directions in which the work develops – I treat these terms with some caution. So, as well as placing the balance towards a more conceptual engagement, the second solution I adopt is to find this broader social context by turning to work that provides such a vision from across the social sciences and humanities. I attempt to work here with materials that are not often used in understanding culture and media but which are of great value in revealing things about power, infrastructures, mobility, place, capitalism and the like. I turn to these to build a material and everyday vision of new media and popular culture in this wider and more situated context.

As a final note, and to further situate the text that follows, there has been much written over the last few years about the problems and opportunities that are presented to the social sciences and humanities by the profusion of vast amounts of digital data – or what is sometimes rather optimistically called 'big data' (boyd and Crawford, 2012). There has been a good deal of prevaricating about what this means for social and cultural research. The focus has tended to be upon the scale of new forms of social data that are now out there, and how we might use such data to tell new types of stories about the social world. The worry has been over how we might access and cope with such a deluge of data, and even with how we might compete or demarcate our own analytical value in such a context of data, data play and predictive analytics (Abbott, 2000; Savage and Burrows, 2007). This is all fine and necessary, but I think we are missing something in these debates. We lack a developed understanding of what these new 'digital' social data are, how they form, how they accumulate, how they are organised, how they circulate and how they feed back into culture. In short, we know little about the data themselves or about the politics, infrastructures and agendas that underpin them. By focusing upon popular culture, as the site in which much of these data are generated and incorporated, we can begin to reflect upon these questions and in turn build a clearer picture of what these data are and how they are manifested. This is not a book about data and social research methods, but let me begin by suggesting that it can be read as a book that is intended to speak to some of these debates. It is here, in answering such a set of questions, that we might be able to make a distinctive contribution, a contribution that competes with the social and cultural analysis that is going on all around us (Beer and Burrows, 2010b). At the same time, this will also allow us to make more informed judgements when we come to respond to, critically analyse or work with such data. Let me put these debates to one side and focus now upon the substantive exploration of the book's core themes.

The structure and content of the book

Following this brief introductory chapter, the book moves through a series of different areas or analytical dimensions that are located at the intersections of popular culture and new media. The book starts out from broad accounts of the infrastructures in which popular culture and new media come to intersect in everyday life, and then moves from this broad scale towards increasingly more localised forms of analysis. To give an opening impression of the different scales of analysis at stake, let me briefly now provide an overview of the content of the book and foreground some of its key arguments.

As mentioned, Chapter 2 begins by developing a broad conceptual account of the context in which the book is set. It takes objects and infrastructures as its focus and offers a foundational account of the key points of reference that open up the possibility for a more material engagement with culture. This chapter looks at the type of conceptual and analytical resources that might be used to analyse the everyday infrastructures within which popular culture and new media converge. It focuses upon the objects and infrastructures that facilitate the capture of these new forms of data (and in turn also then make their circulation possible). In order to do this, it draws upon a range of sources to work through from objects, to infrastructures and then to assemblages. The specific properties of contemporary objects and infrastructures are outlined here. The chapter turns to the work on urban infrastructures, and suggests that this work might be used in various ways to contextualise cultural analysis. Alongside this, the chapter also explores Manuel DeLanda's (2006) assemblage theory and suggests that we might be able to use such analyses to understand the complex material assemblages of popular culture.

The chapter explores how the infrastructures that form the backdrop to everyday life draw out new forms of data. It calls upon Dodge and Kitchin's (2009) concept of 'logjects' as a mechanism for understanding how these mobilities are captured, sorted and relayed by the devices that we routinely deploy across the spaces of everyday life (we return to the combination of data, devices and bodies in Chapter 6). The notion of logjects is used to understand how data can be extracted from moments of cultural engagement. This chapter is used to argue for an appreciation of the material underpinnings that facilitate and constitute contemporary popular culture. It argues that in order to fully understand contemporary culture we need to develop a greater understanding of the systems and flows that shape what it is. The argument of Chapter 2 is that we need now to write these objects and infrastructures into cultural analysis. The chapter closes by reflecting upon the notion of cultural assemblages and how this notion might be used in developing cultural analysis. These observations provide the foundation and conceptual backdrop for the following chapters.

Sticking with this infrastructural and broad focus, Chapter 3 looks at the archive and archiving. It uses the concept of the archive for thinking through the organisation and ordering of culture. It is concerned with how new media archives are the site of everyday forms of cultural engagement. Once data has been generated and extracted, it is often categorised and archived. This chapter looks at the processes of archiving in popular culture, and suggests that this can be used to reveal the organisation and self-organisation of cultural circulations. The concept of archives can be used as a way to understand how by-product data are organised in culture, who controls them, what is stored, how it is accessed, how it is managed and so on. Using the concept of archives allows us to see these processes more clearly by focusing the analysis upon the ways in which data are held, directed, searched or accessed.

The chapter begins by developing the notion of archives both historically and conceptually. Mike Featherstone's work on the archive is crucial in understanding the way that archiving has become central in contemporary culture. Within his broader discussions, Featherstone (2000) talks about the way that the walls of the archive have stretched around everyday life. This chapter looks to explore this notion further in order to elaborate some specific examples of archives in everyday popular culture. The chapter returns first to the informational infrastructures from the opening chapter, and expands upon the types of infrastructures that extract data and how these have become embedded in everyday routines: what I describe here as the *infrastructures of participation*. Further to this, Chapter 3 points towards the need to understand not just the infrastructures of participation but also the infrastructures of participative organisation and ordering.

The book's focus then shifts towards some of the underlying ordering forces within these infrastructures. Chapter 4 looks at how software algorithms are shaping the formation of cultural tastes and experiences. The chapter opens with a discussion of recent work on the social significance of software algorithms. It then looks at some of the emergent debates that, in a number of ways, describe how algorithms are coming to 'enact' and 'constitute' the social world in different ways. From this work the chapter develops the key issues around enactment, derivatives, sorting and prediction. The central argument of this chapter is that algorithms are now coming to intervene in the shaping of cultural encounters. This has yet to be fully explored. As such there is a need for cultural analysis to appreciate the part that algorithms now play in cultural formations as they come to manipulate the circulations of popular culture. There is some reason here to explore how the ontology of taste formation is changing under these conditions. The chapter suggests that this tends to be absent in cultural sociology and cultural studies, where taste formations tend to be understood as being the product of social networks, friendship groups and even class positions. We need to begin to move towards an understanding of the part that data flows play within these social connections and groupings as cultural tastes are created and fostered. For example, this chapter asks what it is that enables cultural clusters to form and how these might be appreciated differently if we begin to factor algorithmic power into the analysis.

The move then is towards trying to understand how these infrastructures become a part of everyday cultural practices. Chapter 5 attempts to do this through the concept of *data play*. One of the most visible forms of data folding back into popular culture occurs where web users play with the data. This chapter treats this data play as a continuum activity that ranges from relatively passive forms, such as an interest in seeing 'what is hot', with real time charts and online aggregators, through to more extreme and active forms of engagement, where individuals use various data sources to create sophisticated visualisations of culture and to open up new possibilities for cultural engagement. This chapter argues that these new forms of cultural engagement are made possible by *the circulation of data about culture*. These transformations have some important outcomes for popular culture. We begin with the general notion that popular culture is speeding up, as we begin to see in real-time what is happening and what is 'trending'. Alongside this we can begin to see a kind of 'social factory' (Gill and Pratt, 2008) emerging in popular culture, where this data play is at its most active in creating products, visuals and web resources. Finally, the chapter attempts to categorise the different types of data play that can be observed and looks at how these perform a role in circulating data. These forms of data play enable the feedback loops, as John Urry (2003) has put it, of culture to emerge. These cultural feedback loops are actually now central in the consumption of music, games, visual materials and the like. This chapter argues that we need to take these various forms of data play seriously as they are now at the centre of the relations, communication and dissemination of popular culture. They are shaping how people find culture, how they view it and how they communicate these thoughts to other individuals.

The final substantive chapter of the book, Chapter 6, continues to locate the everyday within these infrastructural intersections of popular culture and new media. It considers how the body might be placed into these broader new media infrastructures and cultural assemblages. It positions the body within the systems and flows of data discussed in the previous chapters. In this chapter the body is re-inserted into the analysis as an inextricable component part of these circulations of culture. It opens with some reflections upon a broader literature that has argued for the need to include the body in social and cultural analysis; the purpose of this is to look to establishing the importance of connectivity between media, emotions and the body in the analysis. This chapter suggests that the connections and 'boundary conditions' between bodies and informational infrastructures represent the sites within which culture is occurring. Interfaces are the sites of the connections between bodies and information, the places where, as Hayles (1999) has argued, information is 'instantiated' as culture. As such, and returning to the argument of Chapter 2, we need to understand how everyday devices come to shape what culture is and how it interfaces with the time and space of everyday life. Chapter 6 takes mobile devices and the production of affective bodily territory as its focus.

The book then concludes with a more explicit version of the argument that circulations are central to popular culture, and that we, therefore, need to gain a greater understanding of the systems that facilitate these flows if we wish to gain a greater understanding of contemporary culture. The conclusion illustrates how the concepts and ideas discussed in the previous chapters fit together in the analysis of culture. This section is also used to open up the missing dimensions of the analysis offered in the text, and to suggest that such an approach requires a more continuous and sustained focus upon the materiality and material dynamics of everyday culture. The conclusion suggests that the *doing* of culture has changed, so the ontology, and some of our assumptions about culture and our existing methods and concepts, might need to be rethought in this light. The book closes with some thoughts on what this might mean for how we proceed with an analysis of culture.

This brief opening outline then is intended to give an impression of how the book's content and structure works. In short, the book looks through a series of analytical dimensions – starting from objects and the broader infrastructural assemblage and working through, archiving, algorithms, data play and to the body – in order to see the way that popular culture and new media intersect in the context of everyday life. I hope that this will be provocative and that highlighting these new dimensions will be illustrative of the way that culture works today. It is also hoped that as the chapters develop the reader will see the types of problems and opportunities that these different dimensions create for the study of culture more generally. Let me begin then, in the next chapter, by situating this book in some wider analytical streams and by beginning to outline the kind of conceptual framework that is needed to perform the task at hand. We begin with the component objects and infrastructures of the cultural assemblage.

2
Objects and Infrastructures: Opening the Pathways of Cultural Circulation

Introduction: Placing culture in its material context

The book you are reading might be printed on paper and card, or you might be reading this off some sort of e-reader, a Kindle or maybe an iPad; it could even be that you are reading it on your phone or some other device. Perhaps you are reading this chapter on one of those sites that enables a short preview of some of the content, maybe something like Google books or the preview function on Amazon, or you might even have accessed an illegal PDF. This book is a kind of cultural object, but it is also part of an infrastructure. Behind its production we can imagine publishers, designers, typesetters, editors, proof-readers, digital files, emails, printing presses, paper merchants, distributors, wholesalers, retailers, online shops, postal delivery services or the platforms that allow for web-based access to a virtual text, the list goes on. On top of this you might reflect on how you found my book in the first place. Perhaps you read a review, maybe it was recommended to you by an online retailer, maybe you spotted it on a shelf or you located it through a search interface in a library or online, maybe on Google Scholar, or via a post on some form of social media. In short, this object has formed and been made mobile by an infrastructure.

The point is perhaps a little crude, but the fact is that we cannot really hope to understand culture unless we begin to see it in the context of these objects and infrastructures. It is not realistic to imagine that we can capture this complexity in the round, but it is feasible to think about some of these material dimensions and how the altering form of our everyday objects and infrastructures may implicate and be implicated by culture.

To this end, this chapter, as I have already indicated, is intended to provide something of a contextual and conceptual backdrop for the chapters that follow. I start here by laying out a broad conceptual framework that will set up the more specific chapters that follow. The chapter moves through three stages in this process. First, it begins with *objects*. It describes the nature and role of objects in everyday life and looks not just at how memory and meaning are attached to objects by people, but also how new types of objects now have their own capacity to remember their use, activities and movements. The second stage moves away from individual objects and towards the broader *infrastructures* of which they are a part. In this section, a range of work on the materiality of space and information is used to show the necessity for thinking infrastructurally about culture, particularly where these infrastructures come to have a constitutive set of implications for culture and how it is encountered. Then, third and finally, the chapter attempts to bring these objects and infrastructures together, along with bodies, culture and data, through the concept of the *assemblage*. In short, the chapter works towards an approach that analyses culture by placing it within this cultural assemblage. The point of this approach is to show how different dimensions and scales might be necessary in order to generate a more complete understanding of culture as it is today. Thinking in terms of objects, infrastructures and assemblages enables a material encounter with these different cultural dimensions and opens up an analysis of the intersections between popular culture and new media. The central objective of the chapter is to begin to make visible what might be thought of as the material pathways of cultural circulation.

Objects

It is probably something of an understatement to say that you could write an entirely separate book about 'objects'. Indeed, the wealth of material in this area could take you on a tour through vast swathes of philosophical, anthropological, archaeological, historical and socio-logical work. In sociology alone, which of course will draw on earlier philosophical understandings of objects, we might turn to Emile Durkheim's later work, or Georg Simmel's essays on the materiality of the ordinary, or we could work through to the contemporary mobilities turn (Urry, 2007) or the current interest in affect theory (see Chapter 6). In contemporary philosophy, for instance, we might be drawn towards an engagement with object-oriented philosophy and its concern with the analysis of an 'object-oriented ontology' (for a recent discussion see Bogost, 2012). Within this work, and without wanting to get pulled into the midst of too many of these numerous debates, I would like to carve a very particular furrow. My concern here is with identifying some of the distinctive qualities of contemporary objects. In particular though what I would like to do in this section is to reflect upon the relations between objects and memories. It is here that we can identify an important shift from the way that objects evoke memories and towards objects that have their own capacity to remember. We still, of course, attach our own memories to objects, but rather, over time, objects that capture something of their use have become embedded in everyday life and have come to mediate a number of forms of cultural engagement.

Let us begin with the way that objects evoke or stimulate emotional responses or memories of times and places. Walter Benjamin's (1999a) essay 'Unpacking my library' focuses upon the importance of the material properties of books. Benjamin's essay describes the nature of his relations with his book collection as he unpacks his books from a storage crate. Benjamin raises a number of issues, but underpinning the piece is the part that the book – not just as a text but as material object of paper, card and so on – plays in the fostering of memory. Central in this is the connection between the biography of the individual, or the collector as he puts it, and the biography of the object. Benjamin points towards us having a material biography within these everyday objects. Benjamin's essay explores this important set of tacit connections between our own biographies and the material objects that populate our lives. Previously I attempted to use Benjamin's piece to think about how the nature of cultural objects has changed and how our relations with material culture might also ultimately be altered. The first piece (Beer, 2008a) questioned the rise of what are often thought of as 'virtual' objects, such as MP3 and other digital compression formats, and asked what this might mean for the type of material biographies that Benjamin described. The second piece (Beer, 2012a) used Benjamin's essay to suggest that we might need to think about the nature of our relations with mobile media devices as material objects, to think about how such attachments might simply move between different media – with iPods, iPhones, iPads, Kindle and the like having the material properties that we still see as a part of our biographies.

The notion that objects provide an evocative presence in our lives is something that has been explored by a range of thinkers. For example, Sherry Turkle's recent edited volume on what she describes as 'evocative objects' is a useful starting point. In framing the collection, Turkle (2007: 5) says this:

> We find it familiar to consider objects as useful or aesthetic, as necessities or vain indulgences. We are on less familiar ground when we consider objects as companions to our emotional lives or as provocations of thought. The notion of evocative objects brings together these two less familiar ideas, underscoring the inseparability of thought and feeling in our relationships to things. We think with the objects we love; we love the objects we think with.

Again, Turkle's collection, like Benjamin's piece, is not concerned with the actual functionality of the object but with the importance of its material presence in that individual's life. By way of situating the various pieces in the collection, she adds that:

> there has been an increasing commitment to the study of the concrete in a range of scholarly communities. To this conversation, *Evocative Objects* contributes a detailed examination of particular objects with rich connections to daily life as well as intellectual practice. Each author has been asked to choose an object and follow its associations: where does it take you; what do you feel; what are you able to understand?
>
> (Turkle, 2007: 7)

Turkle's collection then is an attempt to show how 'evocative' these ordinary objects might be, to show how they are embedded in everyday practices and understandings. The aim is to see what it is that they evoke and how they are a part of a biography and the materialisation of memory.

Turkle is not alone in her attempts to uncover such connections and relations. Published at around the same time as Turkle's (2007)

Evocative Objects, and thus offering some support for her observation about theoretical trends in the study of 'the concrete', we find two other books that contain parallel discussions of how 'evocative' objects can be. The first, edited by Joshua Glenn and Carol Hayes (2007), is a similar type of collection to Turkle's in that it contains various reflections on personal evocative objects. The second was a single authored book that attempted to understand the role of these objects in the life of the author (King, 2008). Alongside this, we have collections, such as that edited by Costall and Drier (2006), that attempted to understand these relations from a design perspective – for a particular example see the essay on 'The cognitive biography of things' by David de Léon (2006). And for a more programmatic and comprehensive set of observations on the use and importance of objects in the negotiation of everyday life, and particularly as an evocative source of memory and emotion, we can turn to Daniel Miller's detailed works exploring the part that 'things' play in the lives of the residents of a street (Miller, 2008) or his more general observations on the role of 'stuff' (Miller, 2010; and for a brief overview of the above literature see Beer, 2012a).

This would suggest perhaps, that the connection between objects and memory is based upon the individual's placing of the object within moments, events or emotional times in their lives. The material biography here is about this very personal understanding of the object and its meaning for the individual as they engage with it. The memory here is on the part of the human agent, who looks through the object into their own past or who has some emotional response to the object based on their understanding of it. In this opening section of this chapter though, we are also interested in how the objects themselves develop a kind of memory. This is a question of how the object can capture aspects of its use, as an inscription, that might have meaning beyond the individual. For Benjamin, the object always captured its history of use in its particular auratic qualities, the marks on it, the sun damage, the curling of pages, the yellowing of paper, the scuff marks, the aromas and so on. So there was a capturing of something of the biography of that particular object. The difference is that this was inscribed on the physical form of that object rather than being extractable as data. It is a less retrievable history of use that can probably only really be fully elaborated by the owner's unique understanding of these indelible marks, made as they are where the biographies of the object and its owner intersected. This physical inscribing of the object's history on its form still exists, but the difference now is that many objects also actively capture data about their use that can then be extracted and used in various ways.

Writing back in 2005, the science-fiction author turned design futurist Bruce Sterling wrote a short manifesto for emergent objects. The book elaborated some detailed accounts of the changing nature of technological objects culminating in the concept of 'SPIME'. SPIME, he explained, were emergent objects that were beginning to come into existence but which would come to be much more prominent over the coming years. This book was a work of design futurism concerned with imagining the types of objects that, according to Sterling, were soon to be with us. As Sterling described:

> 'SPIMES' are manufactured objects whose informational support is so overwhelmingly extensive and rich that they are regarded as material instantiations of an immaterial system. SPIMES begin and end as data. They are designed on screens, fabricated by digital means and precisely tracked through space and time throughout their earthly sojourn.
>
> (Sterling 2005: 11)

This fed, at the time, into debates about what was called the 'internet of things'. The crucial point being that objects were increasingly connected, sometimes taking material or physical forms, and sometimes existing as data or information (Gane and Beer, 2008: 35–52). SPIME would be the types of objects that could be tracked and traced. They had, or have, a unique reference identity that can be followed through their history, and similarly the component parts making up that particular SPIME could also be tracked back to their origins. Thus, for Sterling, this complicates the separation between physical and virtual objects. Rather, it foretells the rising connectivity of things and the increasing trackability of objects (for a more detailed discussion of Sterling's contribution see Beer, 2007a).

Some years have passed now since Sterling's book was published and we might begin to see some merit in his futurism. We can begin with a technology that Sterling himself points to as an early form of SPIME: the RFID or Radio Frequency Identity tag. RFID tags have attracted quite a bit of interest from sociologists and geographers, especially those who are interested in the connectivity of things and spaces in information dense environments (see for example Thrift, 2005; Mitchell, 2005; Beer, 2007a; Crang and Graham, 2007; Hayles, 2009; Kitchin and Dodge, 2011; amongst others).

It is probably quite well known by now that many consumables have embedded tags, or RFID tags. Much packaging and the like contains such devices. This is unlikely to be news by the time you come to read this book. But these tags are important because they intimate towards the increasing networking of objects, spaces and even bodies (see Beer, 2007a and Chapter 6). In a dedicated article on these devices Katherine Hayles (2009: 48) argues that:

> From the beginning, RFID technology has been entangled with politics...Surveillance remains one of the principal concerns raised by RFID technology, now so small and cheap that it can be embedded in a wide variety of products and objects. More subtle, but no less important, are the effects of RFID in creating an animate environment with agential and communicative powers...the political stakes of an animate environment involve the changed perceptions of human subjectivity in relation to a world of objects that are no longer passive and inert.

RFID tags then have been seen as being an embodiment of an 'ontological' change brought about by the rise of information dense environments in which agency is challenged by thinking things and spaces (see Chapter 4), or 'thoughtful territories' as I have called them elsewhere (for an overview see Beer, 2007a). RFID tags, according to Hayles, are representative of the broader 'movement of computation out of the box and into the environment' (Gane et al., 2007: 349). Elsewhere, Mackenzie and Vurdubakis (2011: 16) describe a 'concern with how codes and codings "work" by endowing their objects with being'. I'll return to the issues of agency and bodily interfacing raised by Hayles in chapters 4 and 6 in particular, but for the moment it is simply worth pointing towards the nature of these changing environments in which connectivity is being facilitated by the newly networked objects. As Hayles puts it in an interview from around the same time, if 'the relational databases are the brains of the system, RFID tags are the legs' (Gane et al., 2007: 349).

More recently we can look beyond RFID and towards more complex objects that perform more detailed forms of data extraction. This category of objects has been described by Dodge and Kitchin (2009) as 'logjects'. Amongst a range of objects that now require code to function (see also Kitchin and Dodge, 2011), Dodge and Kitchin focus upon the most developed, the 'logject'. They describe these objects in the following terms:

> Logjects... record their status and usage and, importantly, can retain these logs even when deactivated and utilise them when reactivated. In key ways these logs can have a bearing on the on-going operation of the object and its relations with people or wider processes... We broadly define a 'logject' as an object that monitors and records its own use in some fashion.
>
> (Dodge and Kitchin, 2009: 1350)

Previously I have provided a detailed account of how the concept of the logject might be applied to mobile music devices (see Beer, 2010a; and for a general overview of the conceptualisation of objects and spaces see Burrows and Beer, 2013). This earlier piece provided a specific account of the cultural application of logjects. For the moment though it is worth reflecting simply on what Dodge and Kitchin's formulation might reveal about the nature of the contemporary objects that populate everyday spaces. The above excerpt indicates that 'logject' is a collective classification for objects that capture details about their use as data; these data are then stored and can be accessed by the relevant organisations. Thus the object becomes an active and crucial part of the functioning of 'knowing capitalism' (Thrift, 2005) and of the connectivity of the environment observed by Hayles and others. We can imagine then how such devices, which are often central in our engagements with popular culture – iPods, iPads, laptops, smart phones and so on – are active in capturing aspects of our everyday lives and our cultural engagements. These objects also then become the sites within which these data can be fed back in recursive loops to shape our consumption patterns (see Beer, 2010).

The image here is of an environment that is populated by objects that capture details of their history and make these available for extraction. Dodge and Kitchin (2009) add some further detail to the broader category of logjects by identifying two types of logject. The first is the 'permeable logject', which captures and stores data which is then retrieved when the device is connected up to another networked device. The second is the 'networked logject', which again stores the data but which is constantly connected into the environment. This then begins to give a sense of how the nature of objects and environments might be altering, with the emergence of new types of networked or connected objects. Alongside this, with RFID we see the potential for all objects to be connected and tracked in different ways and for the environment, through such objects, to become increasingly connected. Of course, this is only part of the picture, it does not focus upon how older and more traditional objects interface with such practices and developments (sometimes as acts of resistance to the motif of connectivity). But we can see how these 'logjects', as I have partially shown elsewhere (Beer, 2010) and which I hope to develop in this book, are often likely to be at the centre of the intersections between popular culture and new media. We might note with some certainty, for example, that there is a layering of different types of memory at these intersections.

All of this is before we even begin to open up the range of different types of objects that might be elaborated upon. If we hope to develop a more detailed picture, we would also need to think broadly of other emergent objects at the intersection between popular culture and new media. These objects would include virtual compression formats and the digital objects that they create, such as the MP3 file, which has been explored in some detail as a contemporary object by Jonathan Sterne (2012). We could also note the rise of brands, which Lash and Lury (2007) have described as 'objects' that can be tracked through the mediascape and which are central to the flows of global capitalism and the general 'mediation of things' (and for an earlier working of what happens to objects in an 'information age', see Lash, 2002: 49–64). Taken together, these indicate that at the intersection and points of connection between popular culture and new media we might find a complex integration of emergent objects, including digital formats, mobile devices, trackable sensors and reified brands, alongside old media and old formats. There is a need, given the connectivity of the objects that are being accounted for, to see these objects as a part of their broader infrastructures.

Infrastructures

In his programmatic book on *Mobilities* (2007), John Urry indicates that part of the value of a focus on mobilities is that it enables us to see the power of infrastructures as a new analytical territory within the social. Urry's (2007: 19) point is that 'social science mostly focuses upon the patterns in which human subjects directly interact together and ignores the underlying physical or material infrastructures that orchestrate and underlie such economic, political and social patterns'. We can perhaps extend this out to cultural patterns. But this is quite a lofty ambition and is fraught with difficulties. Not least of which is the visibility of such infrastructures. Geoffrey Bowker and Susan Leigh Star (1999: 33), who we return to in Chapter 3, have observed that 'a good infrastructure is hard to find'. Their point being that the more integrated the infrastructure the less noticeable it is. In this way, infrastructures have the capacity to feel natural. Bowker and Star indicate how difficult it is to understand and analyse complex contemporary infrastructures, dependent as these infrastructures are on the various types of specialist knowledge required to appreciate the various work that they do. This is exacerbated, they claim, by the matter of density, as the 'many layers of technology accrue and expand over time and space' (Bowker and Star, 1999: 33).

Concerns with understanding the social power and ordering forces of infrastructures can be tracked back across various lines of sight. To pick two influential voices as a starting point, and to contextualise this endeavour we might start with Michel Foucault and Walter Benjamin. These two writers had very different concerns and styles, but we can still see an interest in the power of infrastructures in their work. In a chapter focusing upon Foucault in 1976, for example, Stuart Elden (2007b) provides an insight into Foucault's collaborative projects of the time. From the archives, Elden locates an abandoned project in which Foucault intended to examine the 'green spaces' of Paris, which were notable in their general absence. The consequences of this appear to have been of some interest. This fitted into Foucault's broader spatial concerns and interests (see Crampton and Elden, 2007). In the case of Benjamin the materiality of infrastructures, of course, took centre stage in some of his most well-known works. Aside from a wide range of essays in which Benjamin describes the experiences of various city spaces (see Gilloch, 1996), his famous *The Arcades Project* (1999b), which was unfinished at the time of his death in 1940, attempts to capture the very material infrastructures of the Paris arcades as they blend together the forces of modernity with the experiences of everyday life. The eclectic 'convolutes' in Benjamin's collection gather together wide-ranging references to the structures and materials, amongst other aspects of these scenes, which make up the arcades.

If we were going to explore the notion of infrastructures and how they might be understood more fully than is practical here, then we would of course look to these two thinkers as a resource, and we would need to cast the net quite wide. What we see in these writers, and elsewhere, is that infrastructures can be the material instantiation or embodiment of some wider social and political movements (see Harvey and Knox, 2012; Harvey, 2012). The work on the 'restructuring' of urban space as a consequence of neoliberalisation is an instructive example here (see for instance the mentions of infrastructures in Brenner and Theodore, 2002). Given that such an elaboration is not really appropriate here, let us take this general theme and focus more narrowly upon the material infrastructures in which popular culture and new media intersect. To get at the layering of technologies that Bowker and Star mentioned it is helpful to keep this logic of recovery and to turn to the more recent literature that deals directly with contemporary infrastructures.

It would appear that contemporary infrastructures have become so complex that they defy any universal or complete understanding or comprehension. Focusing upon the analysis of this density in urban infrastructures, Graham and Marvin (2001: 8) point out that:

> cities and urban regions become, in a sense, staging posts in the perpetual flux of infrastructurally mediated flow, movement and exchange...The constant flux of this urban process is constituted through many superimposed, contested and interconnecting infrastructural 'landscapes'. These provide the mediators between nature, culture and the production of the 'city'. There is the 'electropolis' of energy and power. There is the 'hydropolis' of water and waste. There is the 'informational' or 'cybercity' of electronic communication. There is the 'autocity' of motorized roadscapes and associated technologies. And so on. Importantly, however, these infrastructural 'scapes' are not separated and autonomous; they rely on each other and co-evolve closely in their interrelationships with urban development and with urban space.

The vision that Graham and Marvin build is of a vast set of interweaving urban infrastructures, built upon various types of interdependencies. This is a vision of a complex networked place that relies upon an increasingly dense and complex infrastructure and set of infrastructural processes. The question they ask then is 'How ... can we imagine the massive technical systems that interlace, infuse and underpin cities and urban life?' (Graham and Marvin, 2001: 8). This is obviously no simple question. And it is not dissimilar to the type of questions asked of infrastructures by Bowker and Star (1999; and see also Chapter 3). It is also a question that might guide an analysis of culture, if we begin to think about the nature of cultural infrastructures of various types and how they might be unpicked and analysed. It is in response to this question about the nature of urban infrastructures that Graham and Marvin develop the notion of 'splintering urbanism'. This notion gets at the difference between ideal visions of infrastructures and the more fragmented forms that these infrastructures often take. As they put it:

> To describe the dialectical and diverse sets of processes surrounding the parallel unbundling of infrastructure networks and the fragmentation of urban space we use the umbrella term 'splintering urbanism' ... We have shown how standardised public or private monopolies, (at least ostensibly) laid out to offer broadly similar services ... are receding as hegemonic forms of infrastructure management. In a parallel process, the diverse political and regulatory regimes that supported the roll-out of power, transport, communications, streets and water networks towards the rhetorical goal of standardized ubiquity are, in many cities and states, being 'unbundled' and 'splintered' as a result of a widespread movement towards privatization and liberalization.
>
> (Graham and Marvin, 2001: 382)

The notion of splintering urbanism, although directed at the city in its focus, is actually a corrective aimed more broadly at idealised notions of networked spaces and joined-up connectivity. A corrective then that we might quite easily begin to see to be of some use in understanding the way that new media operate. In the case of new media, there is a possibility that we could quickly be seduced by idealised visions of connectivity and interfacing making-up complete and perfect networks (Gane and Beer, 2008: 15–33). We might imagine, as is covered in part by the informational focus of some of Graham and Marvin's analysis, that new media are also the site of unbundling and splintering of various types – with consequences then for how it mediates culture. The corrective offered by Graham and Marvin has been developed elsewhere by Stephen Graham. In particular, Graham's (2010a) edited collection *Disrupted Cities: When Infrastructure Fails* and his co-authored article on maintenance (Graham and Thrift, 2007) focus upon developing this corrective to an ideal vision of infrastructures and how they work, and instead look at the problems, the failings and the fragmentation. Graham (2010b) has further extended this through his work on militarisation and the vulnerability of urban spaces, and in his collected work on the interweaving of information and concrete infrastructures (Graham, 2004a).

What Graham's (and his collaborators') work illustrates, is an increasing density to the types and forms of infrastructures with which we are surrounded. We know that these infrastructures, including new media infrastructures, cannot reasonably be thought of as a complete and connected whole, but what are their emergent properties? It is worth reflecting briefly upon one of Stephen Graham's other pieces, this time a collaboration with Mike Crang on the subject of what they call 'sentient cities' (Crang and Graham, 2007). In this piece they maintain this non-idealised notion of infrastructures whilst also sketching out some of the properties of informational infrastructures and the spaces that they remediate.

Crang and Graham (2007: 790) ask, 'what happens to places and people in networked environments where small informational devices and data are brought together – repeatedly, in real-time, and automatically, through systems that sink into the urban background?' This resonates with other images of the sinking of software into the taken-for-granted background of our everyday lives (Thrift, 2005; Amin and Thrift, 2002). These infrastructures then become informational and facilitate various types of data flows. Crang and Graham continue:

> Building on previous work that looks at informational overcoding of environments, usually via geodemographic data, in complex and recursive fashion (…), we suggest that the interaction of data and processing produces new patterns of identification and stratification in place. The identification and locating of people

becomes a key issue. Far from the identity play celebrated for online environments, hybrid spaces enable visibility.

(Crang and Graham, 2007: 790–791)

This is an early attempt then to get at the politics of the emerging urban infrastructures that they observe. We find again that trackability is a crucial issue, which Crang and Graham link into the increased visibility of people and objects. This visibility is not just about the visibility of people though, it is also about the relative invisibility of the infrastructures and infrastructural processes around us – Nigel Thrift (2005) refers to this as the 'technological unconscious' (see also Mackenzie, 2006: 12; Fuller and Goffey, 2012a: 329). Crang and Graham identify a dual play in this infrastructural politics. They argue that the 'politics of visibility, then, emerges both in making technologies visible to us and in how we are made visible to them' (Crang and Graham, 2007: 791). Clearly then the issue of visibility is placed as a crucial issue in these information dense environments, as data is extracted about us, making us visible, by devices that are often familiar, embedded and even sometimes, in the case of coded classification systems and the like, invisible.

The suggestion here is that we are moving towards more active types of environments, where agency becomes more complex and internetworked into the infrastructures in which we live (see Chapter 4; and for an overview see Beer, 2007a). This is not dissimilar to the earlier cyber-futurism of William Mitchell (2003) and his discussions of bodies in networked spaces (I return to this in Chapter 6). For Crang and Graham, the politics of visibility rests within some broader questions about the nature of contemporary infrastructures. Their article suggests that:

> In a world of augmented, enacted, transducted or 'blogjected' space…we will no longer, even if we ever could, be able to see the environment as a mere passive backcloth for social action. At the very least the environment has always recursively influenced and been influenced by action. What these technologies do is to change the temporality of that action…we have…tried to add a sense that environments are now being saturated with anticipatory technologies.

(Crang and Graham, 2007: 811)

I will return to the anticipatory logics of these environments in the discussion of algorithms in Chapter 4, but for the moment we can at least see that there might be a number of questions raised by the nature of contemporary infrastructures and how these shape our environments. It would seem that, following from thinkers such as Donna Haraway (1991), these infrastructures are coming to be more lively and active, and that they are having some constitutive implications for people and places.

One of the most influential sets of voices on these emergent types of infrastructures, which, it should be noted, influenced Crang and Graham's conceptualisation of transducted space, is that of Rob Kitchin and Martin Dodge. I have already discussed their concept of logjects in understanding contemporary types of objects, but this one concept fits into their attempt to think more broadly about how contemporary space works. A range of articles over recent years have culminated in the publication of Kitchin and Dodge's (2011) book *Code/Space: Software and Everyday Life*. At the heart of this book, and building upon their earlier work, is an attempt to work through the details of changing infrastructures and towards a detailed explication of what their core implications might be.

Kitchin and Dodge's (2011) various explorations are framed around the central concept of 'code/space'. They explain that:

> Code/space occurs when software and the spatiality of everyday life become mutually constituted, that is, produced through one another. Here, spatiality is the product of code, and the code exists primarily in order to produce a particular spatiality.
>
> (Kitchin and Dodge, 2011: 16)

The account here is of a recursive or recombinant set of relations between code and space, with infrastructures needing code in order to function. They talk of a kind of 'dyadic relationship between software and space' (Kitchin and Dodge, 2011: x). Fuller and Goffey (2012b: 15) talk of this as being about an 'abstract' form of material infrastructures that are readily open to transformation, thus the infrastructure is not necessarily a fixed point of reference but is itself, because of its form, 'mutable' and open to 'manipulation'.

As these types of infrastructures have expanded and become the backdrop of everyday life so, Kitchin and Dodge (2011) argue, 'code/space' has become more integrated and inescapable. As they describe, it 'is very difficult to avoid the effects – the work – of software in the world, especially in the developed West, because of the difference it makes to the constitution and practices of everyday life. Indeed, to varying degrees, software conditions our very existence' (Kitchin and Dodge, 2011: ix). This notion that code, algorithms and software have come to constitute space is an idea that is finding increasing purchase (for an overview see Beer, 2009a; this issue also reappears in Chapter 4 in particular but throughout the book). Dodge and Kitchin, in the above passage, are almost coming to echo some of the more posthumanist positions of someone like Fredrich Kittler (Kittler, 1999; Gane, 2005), with software able to 'condition' our experiences and even our 'existence'. Again, the liveliness of the infrastructure is highlighted. Stepping outside of these types of spaces is seen to be virtually impossible, with visibility again being identified as an important issue within such infrastructures. Kitchin and Dodge claim that 'even nonparticipation is logged; passivity is as easily monitored by software as activity is' (Kitchin and Dodge, 2011: ix).

Kitchin and Dodge develop the constitutive power of code and the dyadic relations of code and space throughout their detailed book. They frame this in a set of powerful ongoing social processes. For example, in situating their book they contend that:

> Software is thus actively shaping sociospatial organization, processes, and economies, along with discursive and material culture and individuals' construction of identities and personal meanings. And its effects are set to become increasingly pervasive as more and more everyday practices and tasks are augmented or automated by code.
>
> (Kitchin and Dodge, 2011: xi)

These developments are placed then into a series of developments, with emergent properties still coming to unfold as 'code/space' continues to be established within everyday spaces. The importance of acknowledging and responding to this is set out in the closing 'manifesto' that they provide in their book. If these infrastructures are to become more pervasive then it would seem important to begin to think through some of the consequences for various social and cultural spheres.

By way of an illustration of these analytical possibilities, infrastructures are placed by Kitchin and Dodge at the centre of 'code/space' as they come to enable the codification of different types of spaces on various scales. At one point they argue that:

> Given that many of these code/spaces are the product of coded infrastructure, their production is stretched out across extended network architectures, making them simultaneously local and global, grounded by spatiality in certain locations, but accessible from anywhere across the network, and linked together into chains that stretch across time and space.
>
> (Kitchin and Dodge, 2011: 17)

But, for Kitchin and Dodge this is not hyperbole, or 'cyberbole' (Woolgar, 2002), rather they seek to ground this vision in specific contexts, many of which are mundane and ordinary in their scope. In other words, they show how this type of position is not simply rhetoric or an abstract notion of how networked or information society works. They instead look to understand the constitutive power of 'code/space' in specific settings.

In attempting to understand how 'code/space' develops and operates in different settings they work with various conceptual terminologies. They begin with a typology of the types of levels of abstraction that we may need to work at to see these processes in more detail. Their account focuses upon how software is embedded at 'four levels of activity': 'Coded objects' (discussed above), 'coded infrastructures', 'coded processes' and 'coded assemblages'. I do not wish to work this specific typology through in the pages of this book, but we can see that the previous discussion of objects is likely to blend into the analysis (particularly in Chapter 6 but also with 'coded processes' indirectly reappearing throughout the book, but most directly in Chapter 5). For the moment, and to keep with the narrative of this chapter, let us just reflect on their third level of abstraction:

> *Coded Infrastructures* are both networks that link coded objects together and infrastructures that are monitored and regulated, fully or in part, by software. Such coded infrastructure includes distributed infrastructures, such as computing networks, communication and broadcast entertainment networks (mail, telephone,

cell phones, television radio, satellite), utility networks (...), transport and logistics networks (...), financial networks (...), security and policing networks (...), and relatively small-scale and
closed systems such as an individual automobile. The geographical extent of distributed infrastructures varies from the global, as
with satellite-based global positioning systems ... to more localized
coverage, such as a network of traffic lights in a city centre.

(Kitchin and Dodge, 2011: 6)

Again, this scoping of the concept of 'coded infrastructures' is used
to give a sense of the range of forms in which code finds its way into
everyday spaces. Here we quickly see just how embedded these coded
infrastructures are across the spaces of everyday life and also how central coded infrastructures have become to the successful function of
various processes, practices and routines. Coded infrastructures then
are not simply the stuff of hyperbole, they are deeply embedded in
how we live in a range of complex and integrated forms. We simply
could not imagine what would happen if these coded infrastructures
ceased to operate or function. We can also quickly begin to see how
such a formulation might be used to think about how popular culture, through the integration of new media infrastructures in its
production, distribution and consumption, might be understood to
be 'code/space'.

In general terms what we have seen so far is that infrastructures
appear to be more networked, interconnected and potentially splin-
tered. These are infrastructures that rely on code in the constitution
of everyday spaces and processes. Kitchin and Dodge move beyond
infrastructures to try to think about how these 'coded infrastructures'
relate to 'coded objects' and 'coded processes'. They point towards
the presence of a fourth analytical tier, 'coded assemblages'. They
describe these as follows:

Coded assemblages occur where several different coded infrastructures converge, working together – in nested systems or in
parallel, some using coded processes and others not – and become
integral to one another over time in producing particular environments ... These assemblages are much greater than the sum
of their parts, with their interconnection and interdependence

enabling the creation of highly complex systems with high utility, efficiency, and productivity.

(Kitchin and Dodge, 2011: 7)

The level of complexity grows as they attempt then to think of the connections between objects, processes, people and code within assemblages. This, they suggest, is productive in seeing the interdependence and disjunctures. Perhaps then the way to move towards a more nuanced appreciation of the material dimensions of culture, is to explore this observation by Kitchin and Dodge and to draw upon recent debates about the form and merits of the notion of assemblage and assemblages. This in turn might allow us to think through the possibility of a cultural assemblage, parts of which may then be explored in the following chapters.

Assemblages

Couze Venn has observed that 'assemblage' is a concept that is part of a broader raft of concepts that are being used to provide middle range insights into the vast processes of globalisation and modernisation. Venn (2006: 107) observes that the:

> concept of assemblage has emerged as one of a series of new concepts, alongside those of complexity, chaos, indeterminacy, fractals, strong, turbulence, flow, multiplicity, emergence and so on, that now form the theoretical vocabulary for addressing the problem of determination, or process, and of stability and instability regarding social phenomena.

The indication here is of course that some clarity is needed in the use of such a large number of related concepts so that we might see exactly what each has to offer, particularly as they are often, Venn points out, appropriated from the natural sciences. This is especially the case when we find a number of concepts being used to try to understand some of the same types of social and cultural phenomena. We might also wonder, for example, how we might differentiate assemblage from other related concepts, such as 'field', 'network' and 'worlds' (see Bottero and Crossley, 2011), or even going back to consider how the classic 'artworlds' is a kind of assemblage approach (Becker, 1982). Marcus and Saka (2006) draw a similar conclusion in framing the concept of assemblage as part of a broader conceptual vocabulary. They add that assemblage 'is thus a resource with which to address in analysis and writing the modernist problem of the heterogeneous with the ephemeral, while preserving some concept of the structural so embedded in the enterprise of social science research' (Marcus and Saka, 2006: 102). Clearly then we are not looking at a concept that has emerged from nowhere with little baggage. Rather it appears to be part of a general interest in capturing particular heterogenous aspects of the contemporary condition.

In a key work on the topic, Manuel DeLanda (2006: 1) has described an assemblage approach as being broadly 'realist' (see also Anderson et al., 2012a). In terms of the roots of this approach, DeLanda (2006: 3) notes, that:

> A theory of assemblages, and of the processes that create and stabilize their historical identity, was created by the philosopher Gilles Deleuze in the last decade of the twentieth century. This theory was meant to apply to a wide variety of wholes constructed from heterogeneous parts.

DeLanda's key book on assemblage theory, as with his earlier work, looks to translate and develop Deleuze's conceptual frameworks (and for some other suggestions see Marcus and Saka, 2006: 102). The result here is that the assemblage concept has achieved wider recognition in the years since its publication. DeLanda (2006: 3) adds though that it 'may be objected, however, that the relatively few pages dedicated to assemblage theory in the work of Deleuze (much of it in partnership with Félix Guattari) hardly amount to a fully-fledged theory'. DeLanda's project then was to work from these few pages of ideas and to develop and delineate a more detailed conceptual vision of assemblage.

The first thing to note is that the objective of an assemblage approach, for DeLanda (2006: 10), is to see 'wholes characterized by *relations of exteriority*'. What this leads towards is a vision of the whole that is not totalising, but that looks at the parts within the assemblage in order to understand the whole. He adds that these 'wholes are irreducible and decomposable' (DeLanda, 2011: 188). One of the big advantages of such an approach is that it attempts to account for a 'multiscaled social reality' (DeLanda, 2006: 38). DeLanda (2006: 45) claims that 'these specialized assemblages are capable of operating at *multiple spatial scales simultaneously'*. An assemblage approach is concerned, according to DeLanda (2006: 31), 'with the discovery of the *actual mechanisms* operating at a given spatial scale'. So a multiscalar approach is central to understanding assemblages and the relations that constitute them (there are, of course, some echoes here of Latour (2005); see also Marcus and Saka, 2006: 102). DeLanda (2006) outlines these scales in his book by moving from 'persons and networks' right through to 'cities and nations' (and for global assemblages see Sassen (2006) scale is also discussed in more detail in Chapter 6).

DeLanda adds that in addition to this 'exteriority of relations' and to the multiple scales that are implied by assemblages, we can also identify two other dimensions of analysis that define the concept of assemblage (for his detailed explication of the differences between assemblage theory and other more established sociological and philosophical positions, see DeLanda, 2006: 8–46; Marcus and Saka, 2006: 101). DeLanda (2006: 12) explains this in the following terms:

> One dimension or axis defines the variable roles which an assemblage's components may play, from a purely *material* role at one extreme of the axis, to a purely *expressive* role at the other extreme. These roles are variable and may occur in mixtures ... The other dimension defines variable processes in which these components become involved and that either stabilize the identity of an assemblage, by increasing its degree of internal homogeneity or the degree of sharpness of its boundaries, or destablize it.

DeLanda is operating in some fairly tricky conceptual terrain here. But what we might extract from this, is that not only are the exteriority of relations and scales important in the analysis of assemblage, so too are the nature and role of the component parts and the way that they work together to maintain or challenge the internal coherence of the assemblage. In the case of the above passage, we see that these additional two dimensions are used as a heuristic frame for thinking about how assemblages operate, how they are bound together, by what and how their boundaries or perimeters or drawn and maintained. In his later work DeLanda argues that these properties need to be seen in historical terms and within the context of the broader network of assemblages (DeLanda, 2011: 185–186; see also Sassen, 2006). This remains relatively abstract at this point – although DeLanda is careful to apply these ideas in the second half of the book and in the epilogue to his later book (DeLanda, 2011: 184–203). Rather than explore these in more detail, let us shift instead to see what other writers are doing with the concept of assemblages, particularly as the concept has stoked some debate recently in political geography.

Colin McFarlane has played a central part in developing the assemblage debate. Given that it was a foundational source, it is not surprising that the key ideas that McFarlane works with are close to some of those I have outlined from DeLanda's work. McFarlane takes this a little further in exploring how the concept might be used more specifically in critical urbanism (although for an outline of the various uses see Anderson and McFarlane, 2011). Perhaps unsurprisingly McFarlane (2011: 206) suggests that '[a]ssemblage – whether as an idea, an analytic, a descriptive lens or an orientation – is increasingly used in social science research, generally to connote indeterminacy, emergence, becoming, processuality, turbulence and the sociomateriality of phenomena'. McFarlane's (2011: 207) key observation is that assemblage is used to foreground 'a relational process of composition' and that it shifts the focus to interactions, elements and agency. The assemblage, in McFarlane's work, is a starting point for an exploration of the urban imaginary. It, he adds, 'functions as a heuristic, a disposition, a form of thinking from which theory and critique might depart' (McFarlane, 2011: 208).

McFarlane claims that assemblage thinking can make three contributions. These three contributions revolve around the descriptive understanding of the relations that make up the assemblage, the conception of agency and the way that the concept stimulates the critical imagination. As McFarlane (2011: 221–222) explains, assemblage offers three things:

> First, assemblage emphasizes thick description of the relations between history and potential... Second, assemblage distributes agency across the social and the material, and in doing so draws attention to the agency of the materials themselves as processes within assemblages... Third, the imaginary of the assemblage as collage, composition and gathering contains a potential political contribution to... critique.

McFarlane's observations are highly suggestive and indicate some clear value in taking such an approach, not least because it indicates how we might think across objects and infrastructures. It is also suggestive of the need to incorporate processes and practices, and even bodies, actors and the like into our analysis. For McFarlane, the assemblage approach raises questions about the contextual relations that we observe, but it also questions the notion of agency within the specific assemblage (see in particular Chapter 4). Finally, the assemblage helps us to imagine, in heuristic form, these relations and the various components and agencies as they combine and interact. More than this though, it enables us to imagine and therefore creatively open-up various dimensions of the assemblage for analysis.

Clearly then, one of the difficulties is the size of the potential analytical scope of the imagined assemblage. As we have seen, it is an attempt to think of things together, in interrelation, and to work with components within the whole. The result, for Marcus and Saka, is that there:

> is an ambiguity in the referential frames in the uses of assemblage. It can refer to a subjective state of cognition and experience of society and culture in movement from a recent past toward a near future...or it can refer to objective relations, a material, structure-like formation, a describable product of emergent social conditions, a configuration of relationships among diverse sites and things...And of course, if not explicitly delineated, it can refer to all of these at once.
>
> (Marcus and Saka, 2006: 102)

This scope of conceptual possibilities indicates of course that we need to be cautious. We need to be careful to ensure that the concept is not overstretched in the analysis, and to be even more careful in delineating the aspects or dimensions of the assemblage we are working with (Marcus and Saka, 2006: 106). Indeed, it is here that it is helpful to recognise Brenner et al.'s (2011) argument that we need to link assemblage-based approaches into other theories, concepts and methods for it to be productive. In this way, assemblage approaches might give us a general perspective and help to guide us towards forms of multi-dimensional analysis, but at the same time it requires other concepts that help us to delineate properties and boundaries and to navigate the mass of detail that the notion of assemblage is likely to generate. In other words we need other conceptual points of reference to successfully delineate the frame of reference that we are working with. It is by doing this, along with a focus on specificities, that we might lose what Brenner et al. (2011) call the 'decontextualized standpoint' of assemblage approaches and where we might productively be able to work within assemblages and use the concept to bring certain issues, questions or properties to the surface. The general conceptual looseness and the plethora of reference points that assemblage approaches open-up is a limitation, but then again the importance, as McFarlane (2011) notes, is what it helps us to 'imagine'. The scope is necessary. This is what has been described as the open 'ethos of engagement' or the 'ethos of experimentation' that is central to these approaches (Anderson et al., 2012b: 174–176).

The point is that an assemblage approach might help us to imagine, and therefore unravel, a materially situated context to the analysis. It provides ways into the different dimensions of culture. Assemblage thinking brings together objects and infrastructures with bodies, culture and data. The question to consider is how the notion of assemblage might help us to see the material conditions in which popular culture intersects or is mediated by new media. A concept can only do so much work, but it might be beneficial in the possibilities it creates for seeing the various material dimensions and scales within which new media remediate popular cultural engagements. As such, the concept of 'assemblage' need not be applied in a dogmatic way, but it might help us to be sensitised towards some of the dimensions of culture that tend to be overlooked when focusing upon individual agents and communities. It might point us towards a need to see these individuals as a part of an assemblage, placed, as they are, within an infrastructure, and interacting as they are, with objects, structures and individuals. Thinking of the components in these relational structures presents the possibility for illuminating aspects of culture that currently get little attention. This book follows the advice of Wachsmuth et al. (2011) in starting with the 'interpretive dilemma', the intersection of new media with popular culture, and using this as the focus, rather than starting with assemblage as some form of 'ontological foundation' (for an elaboration of this approach in sociology see Gane, 2012a). We, of course, need to be careful to avoid blindly following conceptual trends. The concept of assemblage is used critically here to help us to think across the various material dimensions in which popular culture and media intersect. This could have been done without this particular concept, maybe by using Benjamin, Lefebvre or others, but assemblage is a helpful term in that it enables us to think across some of the dimensions of the social and cultural world that might otherwise be obscured. It also allows us to think about the connections and forms of agency that are at work.

Conclusion: Thinking across and within cultural assemblages

What I have attempted to show in this chapter is the context in which we can imagine and analyse culture as it is today. This, without wishing to get swept away by the rhetoric, is a context within which objects have altered in their scope to capture and remember, to feedback and to actively integrate themselves into patterns of cultural consumption. These objects provide the moments of instantiation within what appear to be complex concrete and informational infrastructures. The result is that we need to now write this material context into the study of culture, and particular popular culture. We cannot really hope to fully understand culture without understanding this material context and its continuities, changes and properties. By looking across a range of work we are able to begin to map out the objects and infrastructures that are at the heart of cultural engagements, and in turn then we might begin to see how they become implicitly embedded in what culture is, how it works, how it is encountered and, as I try to make explicit in this book, how popular culture circulates as it is remediated by new media forms. The vision is that our objects and infrastructures have become more lively. But what is perhaps more important in the context of this book, is that these objects and infrastructures are seen to work together to accumulate data about people, and that this data can then be fed back into practices, behaviours, activities, bodies and even into the form of the objects and infrastructures themselves. We are forced to wonder what this changing infrastructural context might mean for culture, particular as we can imagine that many of these developments are at the very intersections between popular culture and new media that this book aims to explore. The context appears to be one in which cultural encounters, experiences and the doing of culture are occurring within these types of information dense infrastructures and data circulations. These, in general terms, are objects and infrastructures that extract data and allow for it to accumulate and be harvested. We will also see that these are lively environments in which agency is challenged and meshed in various ways.

This then, as I have attempted to describe it in this chapter, is an environment within which culture is being produced, disseminated and consumed. It is within these infrastructures and through these objects that culture is now mediated. In short then, this chapter argues for the necessity to think of a *cultural assemblage.* This is to think of culture within the context of these objects and infrastructures and as they overlap and intermingle with old objects and old infrastructures (see Gane and Beer, 2008). It is by thinking in these terms that we are able to engage with a range of dimensions in the analysis of culture, some of which have been overlooked in the past. Similarly this type of approach allows us to see the connections between these dimensions and to think about what these connections mean for the way that culture is shaped and performed. In short, it allows us to think across the dimensions of the cultural assemblage so that we might identify connections and interrelations. Building upon this as an approach to culture, and in attempting to find the everyday and material properties of culture as they become embodied in the interactions of this cultural assemblage, the book now attempts to open-up some of these dimensions for further analysis. In this instance, I have tried to identify some powerful underlying dimensions in this cultural assemblage and to think about how they might be analysed so as to enable us to open culture up in some potentially revealing ways. This then is to take the general assemblage approach but then to simply identify some key aspects or themes within it, rather than to try to outline the entirety of the contemporary cultural assemblage. Like complexity theory before it (Urry, 2003), assemblage theory can push us towards unfathomable detail and can wrap us up in social chaos and mess. As Katherine Rankin (2011) has pointed out, thick description could combine with assemblage approaches to produce some problematic forms of relativism. In this instance, I have taken some of the key tenets of assemblage theory, but these have been balanced through an interest in particular deployments of objects and infrastructures within these assemblages. This book attempts not to get too bogged down in the vast components of the assemblage, but to look across it to see the important features of these components. The larger project of a cultural assemblage is, of course, something that would need to be pursed across a range of projects given its multiscalar interests and the scope of the analysis it intimates.

As such, the rest of this book can be seen as an attempt to further this notion of the cultural assemblage by focusing upon archiving, algorithms, data play and bodies. These dimensions rest at the heart of the cultural assemblage that I depict here. But these are far from being the complete picture. Indeed, a full analysis of such an assemblage would be programmatic in its scope. Instead what I have tried to do here is to focus on aspects, dimensions or properties that seem to me to be particularly pressing and potentially important. The rest of this book then looks at the intersection between popular culture and new media through the everyday infrastructures and objects that mediate them. Not in its comprehensive totality, but in an attempt to illuminate some key properties that are at the heart of the circulations of contemporary popular culture. It is hoped that by taking this position and by appropriating this range of resources we might be able to open-up the pathways of cultural circulation as they are today. But this now requires us to move from the overarching notions of objects and infrastructures and towards some specific instances. We will begin with the ordering of cultural content, as a large structural issue, before moving through the technical filtering of algorithms and into the practices of the incorporation of data in data play, and close by attempting to situate the body within the cultural assemblage.

3
Archiving: Organising the Circulations of Popular Culture

Introduction: Archiving culture

I've just decided to take a break from writing this chapter. I pick up my guitar and I use my smart phone to access a mobile version of the web resource chordie.com. I search under 'J' and then under 'Je'. I find the band the Jesus and Mary Chain and scroll down to the song April Skies. I find that three people have uploaded their own version of how April Skies can be played on the guitar, this is a part then of a user-generated archive of guitar chords for songs. I pick the one with the highest rating and begin to strum the chords on my guitar. The problem is that I have a little trouble remembering exactly how the melody goes in the second verse. I return to my smart phone and select YouTube, the vast, and again user-generated, archive of video clips. Here again I search for Jesus and Mary Chain and April Skies. I'm confronted with a long list of video clips that have been 'tagged', that is classified by the users themselves, with some or all of the words I have searched for. The list includes various clips of the Jesus and Mary Chain performing April Skies as well as other bands and singers covering the song. I pick a live version of the band performing the song and then join in on my guitar. This is an admittedly banal example, and one that probably reveals more about the author than anything else, but it is nevertheless suggestive of how new types of archives have become embedded in everyday practices. Here from these two archives I was able to find guitar chords and a video performance of the same song, both provided and organised by the users of these expansive cultural archives and their underlying 'impulse' to archive (Featherstone, 2000, 2006).

In fact, the history of cultural production and consumption can be seen as a history of archiving. Even some of the earliest sound production technologies used punch cards and light systems to access libraries of sounds. Sampling also meant that musicians were often dealing with archives in making music. As digital compression formats have taken hold (for an account of MP3 see Sterne, 2012) so the archiving processes have escalated and transformed. And now we have archives of music in places like Spotify that we can stream for free, direct from the archive. Recent developments have presented new ways in which cultural archives are formed, accessed, ordered and maintained. This chapter looks at the processes of archiving in popular culture, and suggests that this can be used to reveal the organisation, and self-organisation, of circulations in popular culture. This chapter looks at the changes that arrive where cultural archiving practices expand into everyday life and as vernacular forms of archiving blend into more official, commercial and organisational structures. The concept of archives can be used to explore the ordering of data in digital culture and to ask who controls them, what is stored, how it is accessed, how it is managed and so on. Using the concept of archives allows us to see these processes more clearly and reveals the stages that allow data to be held or directed in different directions.

The chapter begins by taking a step back to think about the type of classificatory processes that take place in the archiving of culture. It then moves on to explore what archives are, how they can be used to understand cultural formations and how the concept of archiving can be deployed to reveal cultural change in the new *infrastructures of participation*. Taking these observations about classification and archiving as a point of departure, the chapter then focuses upon the act of 'tagging' as an archival and classificatory process. The chapter concludes by arguing that these self-organising archives create questions about cultural hierarchies, encounters and the power of metadata in everyday life settings.

The classificatory imagination

Before delving into archiving it is important to have a sense of the classificatory processes that underpin the organisation and use of archives of various types. At the heart of the archive is the classificatory system or systems that order the content, make it

retrievable and searchable, place it, categorise it and give it meaning. I argue here that we can think of a *classificatory imagination* at
play as archived content is ordered and negotiated (Beer and Burrows, 2013; Beer, 2013). In their influential work on classification,
Bowker and Star (1999) famously argued that classification is a deeply
embedded and routine part of everyday life. 'Our lives' they claim 'are
henged round with systems of classification' (Bowker and Star, 1999:
1). As they put it, to 'classify is human' (Bowker and Star, 1999: 1).
Their depiction of this everyday type of classification is a blend of
formal and informal classification processes occurring through standards and protocols as well as through the ordering practices of
individuals and groups. Bowker and Star (1999: 1–2) point out that
'[n]ot all classifications take formal shape or are standardized in commercial and bureaucratic products. We all spend large parts of our
days doing classification work, often tacitly, and we make up and use
a range of ad hoc classifications to do so.' Bowker and Star's account
is of classification as deeply embedded in routine life. These everyday forms of classification take a variety of forms that range from the
quite rigid and fixed to the contingent and ad hoc. Many of these
go largely unnoticed, familiar as they are and so finely incorporated
into the doing of everyday practices. This gives a sense of the scale of
'sorting' that occurs in these everyday spaces, as existing classificatory
systems are negotiated and as contingent classifications are used to
organise and render manageable various processes or objects as they
are encountered. There is a complex blend then, for Bowker and Star
(1999: 2), of classifications that seem stable and fixed and 'classifications that appear to live partly in our hands'. Their point is that
'we rub these ad hoc classifications against an increasingly elaborate large-scale system of formal categories and standards' (Bowker
and Star, 1999: 6). In other words, our own classificatory systems
sit alongside and come into contact with the larger systems around
them. We can reflect, for example, upon how our own music classifications, the ones we use to organise our music collection or to make
our own playlists, might rub up against those provided by the music
industry, artists and media protagonists. This is the 'fluid dynamics of
how classification systems meet up...a plate tectonics rather than a
static geology' (Bowker and Star, 1999: 31). These are, after all, mobile
classificatory systems with various overlapping interests and ideas.
This is what they describe as the 'practical ontology' of classification
(Bowker and Star, 1999).

The familiarity and ideological incorporation of these sorting processes means that they often go unnoticed, especially as they develop in tacit and emergent ways. According to Bowker and Star (1999: 2–3):

> These standards and classifications, however imbricated in our lives, are ordinarily invisible. The formal, bureaucratic ones trail behind them the entourage of permits, forms, numerals, and the sometimes-visible work of people who adjust them to make organizations run smoothly. In that sense, they may become more visible, especially when they break down or become objects of contention.

These ordering processes remain cloaked by familiarity in our everyday lives, as a kind of unconscious ordering force. There are moments of visibility that occur where this familiarity is jolted by some change or re-categorisation, or where classificatory work becomes the site of disagreement, where classifications no longer fit or work or where the boundaries are sites of disagreement – we only need to search for politically contentious issues on Wikipedia to see such a visibility come into play.

Bowker and Star (1999: 3) wonder though what these largely invisible organising forces are, they pose a set of questions to guide these concerns:

> But what *are* these categories? Who makes them, and who may change them? When and why do they become visible? How do they spread? What, for instance, is the relationship among locally generated categories, tailored to the particular space of a bathroom cabinet, and the commodified, elaborate, expensive ones generated by medical diagnoses, government regulatory bodies, and pharmaceutical firms?... Remarkably for such a central part of our lives, we stand for the most part in formal ignorance of the social and moral order created by these invisible, potent entities. Their impact is indisputable, and as Foucault reminds us, inescapable.

Popular culture is no different. We have little idea of the answers to these question in the sorting of popular culture, and we similarly have little understanding of how classificatory processes work to order culture on commercial, organisational, informal and everyday levels. This is surprising, particularly given how new systems of ordering are now playing out in culture. We are still, to a large extent, working with notions of cultural classification that appear to be unblemished by changes in cultural consumption, production and dissemination (for a case study exploring this in relation to music genre see Beer, 2013). This is the central problem I hope to begin to address in this chapter. It is not that previous accounts of classification in culture are wrong, it is that these accounts are designed to suit the broadcast model of a more centralised mediascape and as such tend to produce quite structured accounts of classification with powerful centralised actors in industry and the like (see DiMaggio, 1987; Lena, 2012). As I describe below, in addressing the questions set out by Bowker and Star, we need to begin to factor in the decentralisation of cultural classification and archiving processes to understand the ordering of culture. In other words we need to develop a stronger sense of the *classificatory imagination* in culture.

To work towards this goal Michel Foucault's (2002) book *The Order of Things*, and more specifically his concept of 'grids' and the 'encoded eye' are instructive. *The Order of Things* is an expansive text that has received a good deal of discussion. I do not want to rehearse the many arguments that this text develops in this chapter, the text itself tells a wide-ranging story of how classificatory systems are powerful in shaping understandings of the world. Instead I'd like to focus on just one of the conceptual formations he offers in the book. Foucault (2002: xxii) makes the following observation on the nature of classificatory processes:

> It is on the basis of this order, taken as a firm foundation, that general theories as to the ordering of things, and the interpretation that such an ordering involves, will be constructed. Thus, between the already 'encoded' eye and reflexive knowledge there is a middle region which liberates order itself: it is here that it appears, according to the culture and the age in question, continuous and graduated or discontinuous and piecemeal, linked to space or constituted anew at each instant by the driving force of time, related to a series of variables or defined by separate systems of coherences, composed of resemblances which are either successive or corresponding, organized around increasing differences, etc.

Foucault points towards a kind of middle ground between the classifications we are surrounded by and how these come to be interpreted. He speaks here of the 'encoded eye', suggesting that we arrive at things with a predetermined understanding of classification that the eye then imposes upon the object. The encoded eye, for Foucault, is the means by which classificatory systems are realised in everyday life, it is the way that classification is interpreted and incorporated into practice. Foucault points to a middle ground in which the encoded eye and reflexive knowledge come together. This suggests that existing classifications are not all-powerful or completely dominant in shaping how we encode the world, but also that we are not free to interpret and classify as we choose. Like Bowker and Star, Foucault points towards this interplay between the classifications around us, what we do with them, and how we might generate our own categories and systems.

This concept of an encoded eye is helpful in imagining how individual interpretations are brought to variously flexible or rigid cultural schemata. In this case though, we might wonder what the resources are that come to inform the encoded eye as it is deployed to classify the objects it observes. The answer for Foucault is that we continually consume what might be thought of as 'grids'. Within these grids we find gaps that can be used to classify and order the things we encounter. As Foucault puts it:

> Order is, at one and the same time, that which is given in things as their inner law, the hidden network that determines the way they confront one another, and also that which has no existence except in the grid created by a glance, an examination, a language; and it is only in the blank spaces of this grid that order manifests itself in depth as though already there, waiting in silence for the moment of its expression.
>
> (Foucault, 2002: xxi)

The processes of differentiation at the centre of classification work as the encoded eye deploys such pre-established grids to slot that thing into a gap. This, in this kind of formulation, is often a hidden or tacit network of boundaries that are routinely deployed to classify the things we are confronted with. The blank spaces of the grid are used, at a glance he suggests, to simplify and order, to categorise and compare. These grids lay dormant, Foucault claims, waiting to be called into action when needed. And when used it is as if they stand for a kind of natural order. These grids then are the resource used by the encoded eye to classify things. The classificatory imagination, as I have called it, operates at the points of tension, as Foucault describes, between the powerful classificatory grids and the attempt to find a middle ground. The classificatory imagination is simply a concept that sensitises us to the processes by which individuals encounter, read and even create new classifications and classificatory systems. The classificatory imagination is an attempt to uncover the way that classificatory systems are used and subverted, adopted and played with, appropriated and reshaped.

The archive and archiving

The above outlines the kind of classificatory processes that are occurring in contemporary culture. These classificatory processes and interests converge with Mike Featherstone's (2006: 595) observation that 'the will to archive is a powerful impulse in contemporary culture'. Featherstone has written two key pieces that have been highly influential in shaping work on the changing archive and how it might be used not just to describe the collection of documents in an official store, but also as concepts for understanding culture and how it is changing (for a detailed exploration of the archive as a concept for understanding contemporary media see Gane and Beer, 2008: 71–86). According to Featherstone the:

> term archive refers to the place where government records are stored. It was initially conceived as the site where official records were guarded and kept in secrecy. The archive was part of the apparatus of social rule and regulation, it facilitated the governance of the territory and population through accumulated information.
>
> (Featherstone, 2006: 591)

This is the kind of traditional image of the archive, housed in official buildings, holding official documents on populations. Guarded. Secret places. With gatekeepers and hierarchies. As such Featherstone points out that there 'is a politics of the archive given its role in grounding authority and the social order and a struggle to turn archives from a private, or restricted access place into one of open access' (Featherstone, 2000: 168). The politics of the archive concern the decisions made about what goes in, how it is categorised and how and by whom it is retrievable. These factors are used to reinforce power structures.

Featherstone is arguing here that archives have been central to the onset of modernity. With archives expanding, he adds:

> People's lives became seen as singularities. They were identified and individuated through their records or file, which were stored as part of a series in the archives. In effect, this was a new form of power, based not on the ideology of individualism, but the actuality of individuation, as whole populations, their bodies and life histories became documented, differentiated and recorded in the archive.
>
> (Featherstone, 2006: 592)

The population in these archives become trackable and observable on an individual level (for a more recent discussion of this see Ruppert, 2011). Instead of a mass of people the archive creates singularities, individuals, whose lives are captured and stored. For Featherstone this is not an abstract notion of individualisation, but is a material separating-out of individual lives. These lives, the bodies and movements, are recorded in these archives in single retrievable files, thus a new type of power developed (see also, of course, Foucault, 1972). Plus, according to Derrida (1996: 17), the archive not only records, but its forms also act to produce events and happenings (for a critical response to both Foucault and Derrida's views on the archive see Gane and Beer, 2008: 71–76).

One of the ways in which the power of the archive works is by shaping memory, it is a particular telling of history and biography as told through the documents it includes or excludes – the archive we might imagine here fits with Walter Benjamin's (1999a: 248) famous assertion that all history is an act of barbarism. Featherstone's point is that the archive is 'a crucial site for national memory' (Featherstone, 2006: 592), and that because of this it is also 'a place for creating and re-working memory' (Featherstone, 2006: 594).

This issue of personal and collective memory then points us towards the new types of archives that are emerging; these are not the rigid and heavy buildings of modernity but are rather to be found in new web cultures and in digital devices of various types (Featherstone, 2006: 595). Archiving now, Featherstone (2006: 594) argues, 'may not just be the activity of the solitary researcher wandering through the scholarly or official archives, but the activity of individuals in everyday life who seek to preserve documents, photographs, diaries and recordings to develop their own archives as memory devices'. In Featherstone's view, these archiving processes have now become a routine part of individual and collective lives. Similarly Jussi Parikka (2012: 114) concludes that '[m]odes of accessing and storing data have changed from centrally governed and walled spaces to distributed and software-based'. He adds (Parikka, 2012: 114) that the 'trash that was trash because of being kept outside the walls gives way to new forms of less official archives in social media. One (wo)man's trash is another's retweet.' The impulse to archive has moved far beyond the state to incorporate all sorts of archives that house myriad documents and other non-text-based resources and keepsakes. These developments trigger all sorts of questions about memory and cognition (Appadurai, 2003; Hayles, 2006). As I write this chapter there is currently a television advert running for Google's new Google+ facility, which encourages the user to store their photos, home videos and other personal documentation in the 'cloud'. This content can be added and categorised and is depicted in the advert as being a lifelong venture, an archive that is permanently there throughout the life of the individual and capturing that biography to be shared with other people. In this case the individual gatekeeper controls what goes in to this personal biographical archive and who it is shared with. This is not stored on any devices or inscribed on any object, but is held out there in the cloud, on unknown servers. Indeed, one of the issues that has been raised about such digital personal archiving is that technologies change and compatibility becomes an issue. Our VHS video tapes, audio tapes and the like become defunct, so it would seem will CDs and other digital media, the suggestion is that cloud computing is permanent and that such compatibility issues will not emerge over time because this material is not stored on a particular format or device. These are personal archives held in the cloud and together form a vast archive of personal biographies held by Google. They are also highly illustrative of Featherstone's (2006) notion of a 'will' or 'impulse' to archive.

Featherstone, who was of course writing before the development of many of the more recent social media or cloud computing based archives, noted that '[t]oday the new information technologies expand our capacity to record everything: to be is to record and to record in volume means to classify, index and archive' (Featherstone, 2006: 595). In other words, as more material is archivable, in order to make it manageable and retrievable from the archive, so too the necessity to organise content escalates. The value of thinking of such developments in terms of archives and archiving is that it forces us to consider how they are organised, structured and ordered. As Featherstone puts it, 'the shifts in the digital archive between flows and classification take us to the heart of the questions about the constitution, formation and storage of knowledge in the current age' (Featherstone, 2006: 596). Perhaps even more than this, it takes us to the heart of the very question of how contemporary culture is constituted, formed, stored and accessed. It seems that such issues need now to move to centre stage in order to fully contextualise our understandings of culture. These archives, and the classificatory imaginations at work within them, are the framework that orders culture in these contemporary media.

It is important then to move towards a more nuanced understanding of what these cultural archives are, how they work and how they are organised. As Geiger et al. have noted, following from Featherstone:

> Recent developments have called conventional understandings of the archive as an organised depository of knowledge administered by gatekeeper-archivists into question. A key contributor to transformation here has been technological innovation, and particularly digitisation, which has for instance opened up the archive to the enthusiastic wanting to post their photos, memories and documents on the internet.
>
> (Geiger et al., 2010: 4)

This echoes Featherstone's earlier observations about the need to broaden the concept of the archive and to understand how these new and emergent types of archives, and the ongoing impulse to archive, play out in a digitally mediated everyday life. Geiger et al. are suggesting that we need to broaden our scope and to think of social media as archives (see also Gane and Beer, 2008: 77–81). This speaks directly to Featherstone's earlier and more general insight that '[r]ather than see the archive as a specific place in which we deposit records, documents, photographs, film, video and all the minutiae on which culture is inscribed, should the walls of the archive be extended and placed around the everyday world?' (Featherstone, 2000: 170). Featherstone couldn't possibly have foreseen how quickly the answer to this question would become such an emphatic 'Yes'. The answer undoubtedly has to be affirmative with the rise of new archives in everyday life, in the forms of highly integrated and massively popular social media and social networking sites that capture mundane life in various ways (Beer, 2008b). As well as Featherstone's archives of the everyday, we might also point here to Osborne's (1999) 'ordinary' archives or Parikka's (2012: 134) 'banal' archives. As Parikka (2012: 134) has observed, '[a]rchiving everyday life is a theme of technological media culture'. Featherstone seemed to spot that we were upon the edge of some changes to the organisation of culture that could be explored through the concept of the archive, a position that has gained further resonance as these changes have unfolded.

The archive unbound and the infrastructures of participation

In a previous book, Nick Gane and I argued that these changes to everyday archives that were predicted by Featherstone, could be thought as an 'unbinding' of the archive (Gane and Beer, 2008: 71–86). This unbinding was twofold. First it was the transformation in the content of the archive, the move was away from the archive as purely textual towards a mixture of text with video, audio and other forms of objects. The means of searching and retrieval have remained largely textual but the contents vary substantially between archives. It is also notable that recent developments in computer science are exploring the possibilities for such archives to be organised and searched through some of these non-textual properties, such as shapes, colours, sounds, movements and the like (Mitall, 2012). On a more popular level, the smart phone app Shazam, which listens to a song and reports on the name of the song and its singer, is an example of how music archives can be searched through audio clips. Second, the unbinding of the archive is concerned with this movement of archives out into everyday life. This is where they are operationalised in everyday life or where they are used to capture and store aspects of the everyday. This is the shift Featherstone described as being from the archive as state or corporate controlled build-ings containing documents, towards more decentralised media-based archives. This unbinding of the archive left open a series of questions. Not least of which is a consideration of what content goes into such archives on the one hand, and how this content is organised on the other.

The content of these unbound archives is often a part and prod-uct of a decentralised mediascape (Beer, 2008b). The fundamental shift here is towards archives that are based upon some form of par-ticipation (which seems now to be the word that has replaced the more dog-eared concept of interactivity, see Gane and Beer, 2008: 87–102). These archives then are the products of what used to be called 'Web 2.0' (Beer and Burrows, 2007), but which is more com-monly referred to as social media. These are much the same thing and despite attempts to create some nuance around such terms (Blank and Reisdorf, 2012), there is a common theme here, which is simply that these are media in which the content is created by what Graham Turner (2010) has called 'ordinary people'. This is a mediascape based upon the productivity of those using it (see Chapter 5). Much has now been written about this type of blurring of production and consumption. A key reference here is Ritzer and Jurgenson's (2010) widely cited article on prosumption as it relates to new web cultures and developments in capitalism. These archives are, of course, the product of 'prosumer' activity, in that the users are not just consum-ing content they are also creating it. Indeed, the obvious blending of production and consumption in these spaces has led to a quite wide engagement with the concept of the prosumer (Beer and Burrows, 2007 and 2010a).

Drawing upon the work of Alvin Toffler, Ritzer and Jurgenson argue that in many ways capitalism has always been based upon prosumption. Yet the conditions, they claim, in recent years have led to an increasing dominance of prosumer activity. According to Ritzer and Jurgenson (2010: 19), the developments they call Web 2.0, but which can be thought of more broadly as the development of the participatory cultures typical of social media, 'should be seen as crucial in the development of the "means of prosumption' (I return to this issue in Chapter 5). These might also be thought of as the *infrastructures of participation*, that is the underlying structures and means by which data accumulates and is ordered and organised. As this picture might inform us, these unbound archives are, as Parikka (2012: 120) has intimated, 'dynamic', they are 'archives in motion'. Earlier archives, he claims, were about 'freezing time' to store and preserve, whereas these are more dynamic and mobile, with changing content and organising classificatory systems and categories. The result is that part of the job of the prosumer, or the capitalist organisation overseeing and attempting to extract value from the prosumer, is the 'continuous maintenance' required by the dynamic archives of social media (Parikka, 2012: 119).

The concept of prosumption is problematic in that it is quite analytically vague, it simply defines a very broad collapsing of boundaries between production and consumption (Beer and Burrows, 2010a). This is quite a crude starting point for analysis, although it should be added that Ritzer and Jurgenson have done a great deal to show how this very broad set of developments have very specific implications for capitalism. We might wonder though what drives such prosumer activity and how it can be understood in the context of everyday practices. On this point Zygmunt Bauman's increasingly influential concept of the 'confessional society' is helpful (Bauman, 2007; Beer, 2008b). Bauman's work steers us towards an understanding of what might then come to populate these archives of 'prosumer' or participative activity. Bauman (2007: 3) observes:

> The teenagers equipped with portable electronic confessionals are simply apprentices training and trained in the art of living in a confessional society – a society notorious for effacing the boundary which once separated the private from the public, for making it a public virtue and obligation to publicly expose the private, and for wiping away from public communication anything that resists being reduced to private confidences, together with those who refuse to confide them.

The first thing to say is that Bauman's focus on teenagers understates the vast numbers of users on social networking sites like Facebook.

The important point here though is that these archives are often confessional, in that they are populated, as Featherstone's earlier argument indicated, with inside information about the everyday life of the contributor. This is not always the case; sometimes the archives are more obviously confessional, such as Facebook, in other instances they capture other types of information, such as the music listened to, as with Last.fm, or the viewpoints on videos on YouTube or celebrity on Perezhilton.com. The key point though for Bauman (2007: 1–24), is the sense of obligation and the fear of being left out that drives the confessional society (see Beer, 2008b). We can imagine, for instance, that a Goffmanesque presentation of self guides the filtering of the confessional content posted on Facebook for instance. The problem is that this might tell us a good deal about the content formed in prosumer acts driven by the demands of the confessional society, but it reveals little about the archives themselves and how they are organised. In other words it reveals something of the participation itself but little about the archives as the infrastructures of this participation.

At this juncture, by way of summary, I would suggest that these archives, embodied in popular web sites like YouTube, Facebook and Flickr, can be thought of as the *infrastructures of participation*. These are the structures in which such participation occurs; these are the spaces, the walls, the formats within which such unbound archives are located (in networked and globalised form). The question to consider then, as I have already indicated, is how these unbound archives are organised, and how these infrastructures of participation are also *infrastructures of participative organisation* or participative archiving.

Tagging, archiving and the classificatory imagination

Earlier in the chapter we spoke of the classificatory imagination. To understand the organisation of these archives and the infrastructure of participative organisation, it is possible to see how the classificatory imagination is active in such archives. The practice of 'tagging' is one of the most powerful organising and ordering practices in contemporary culture, yet it has received very little attention. Tagging is simply the process of labelling content in these archives. So, if we watch a video on YouTube we can label it or tag it with metadata. When content is added, such as a video, the person posting it will usually add tags that describe the content. These tags will then be adorned by others who feel other tags might be needed for the content to be found (or, if the person is feeling subversive, they might also deliberately add misrepresentative tags to the content, which can lead to corrective activity by others). So, if an academic adds a paper of their own to academia.edu they might tag it with 'class', 'capitalism', 'inequality' and the like, thus making it retrievable to anyone searching those key words. Often the cluster of tags that are associated with a particular piece of content can be viewed as a tag cloud, to show those most commonly associated with the content. Similarly whole archives can sometimes be navigated by such word clouds, with the selection of a term producing a list of the content most commonly tagged with that term.

What this brief outline suggests, and because this practice of labelling is so common amongst these new archives, is that tagging is central in understanding the organisation and ordering of contemporary culture. It shapes cultural encounters, it defines how archives work and what is retrievable, and it is the organising principle in these cultural archival spaces. In the opening paragraph of this chapter I located the Jesus and Mary Chain song April Skies on YouTube, I found this version of this song because it had been tagged with the information I was searching for. This is the power of metadata and classification in the archive. In these decentralised archives we find that the infrastructure of participation includes participation in the organisation of the content. This is not an archive with a small number of gatekeepers. It is not just the content that is open but often also the classificatory system underpinning it.

There are of course restrictions and boundaries at work in these archives. Some content is protected. The Facebook profile is an obvious example here. People set their own privacy restrictions on their profiles, so even where someone might be located or a shared taste or preference selected, the content may not be visible because of the privacy settings. Similarly, these sites do have gatekeepers or moderators, sometimes working for the capitalist organisations that extract value from the work of those creating the content. There are restrictions placed on a number of contentious pages on Wikipedia for example. And there are also examples of deliberate attacks on the content of such archives. This means that moderation is sometimes employed, but usually only in quite extreme circumstances. Indeed, often the users of these archives police the content themselves. This indicates that there is some complexity here.

What we find then are powerful questions about the formation of such archives and the ordering of culture within them. These new archives are deeply political spaces, that cannot be simplified with terms like decentralised, democratised or participatory (Beer, 2009b), particularly as they might not only capture culture in the archive and organise it, but also because these 'systems are active creators of categories in the world as well as simulators of existing categories' (Bowker and Star, 1999: 321). The processes of tagging are evidence that 'with the emergence of new information infrastructures, these classification systems are becoming ever more densely interconnected' (Bowker and Star, 1999: 326).

It would of course be a mistake to imagine that these classifications become unconstrained and unanchored simply because they are the products of decentralised media. Cultural 'grids' are not being redrawn by the classificatory imagination simply because the technical affordances of contemporary media make this possible. Rather, we see the type of tensions that Bowker and Star (1999) described as they emerge between existing and emergent classifications. It is often the case, as they argued, that the history of classifications has deep roots and the embeddedness of classification plays a part in the shaping how these archives are ordered. The historically informed 'grid' still informs the 'encoded eye', even where they are faced with multiple or even unlimited possibilities. If we look at any musician for example, on the tag clouds on Last.fm, we are not likely to be too surprised by the labels they are given. This suggests that even with the right technological scope for redrawing cultural grids, there are limiting factors. It highlights in fact that, even with the decentralisation of media and metadata, there is a continuity to cultural classification in these archives. There is inevitably some redrawing of the grids, where the classificatory imagination is at work or where it is creating new categories to describe new aesthetic tendencies or forms, but there is an ongoing power to the cultural grids and the encoded eyes that they inform. The metadata are powerful as they inform the encoded eye, but they are also an elaboration of a new and creative impulse to archive and to exercise a classificatory imagination. What these discussions suggest is that these new archives can be thought of as self-organising. This self organisation creates for us a series of important questions about the power of this new type of organisational metadata in the ordering of contemporary culture.

Self-organising cultural archives and the power of metadata

Scott Lash, in an important contribution to debates on the working of contemporary types of post-hegemonic power, has claimed that '[o]rganization in the older hegemonic politics had to come from the outside... In a post hegemonic politics, there is organization from the inside: there is self-organization... now the brain... is immanent in the system itself' (Lash, 2007: 60). This is a wide-ranging obser-vation, but it applies neatly to the types of archives that we are describing here and that have become typical of popular culture. These can be understood to be self-organising archives that are part ordered by technological non-human actors, as I discuss in the next chapter, and part organised by those involved in using and navi-gating the archive. These are not in the large part archives that are controlled by gatekeepers, although there might be moderator type gatekeepers overseeing the archive, they are often organised by those inside the archive. These then are self-organising archives, archives with an immanent classificatory system produced in the collective classificatory imagination of the users. If the archive concept can be used to provoke questions about ordering and power in cultural struc-tures, then the fact that it is a self-organising system is an important distinction to make. It is also an observation that forces us to con-sider what the power of metadata is in these largely self-organising cultural archives.

Bowker and Star were very clear in their claim that classificatory systems, feeding into archives of course, are deeply political. As they put it:

> We have a moral and ethical agenda in our querying of these sys-tems. Each standard and each category valorizes some point of view and silences another. This is not inherently a bad thing – indeed it is inescapable. But it *is* an ethical choice, and as such it is dangerous – not bad, but dangerous.
>
> (Bowker and Star, 1999: 5–6)

Bowker and Star's book was written sometime before the new classificatory and archiving processes that I have described here, yet the point they make gathers extra weight when we consider how these new archival classificatory systems have expanded to become central in mainstream culture and in the everyday lives of large parts of the global population. Bowker and Star's claim that '[c]lassifications are powerful technologies' and 'should be recognized as the significant site of political and ethical work that they are' (Bowker and Star, 1999: 319) means that we should not overlook the politics of cultural archiving processes and systems. The problem is that such banal instances of everyday routines disappear into familiarity. As Parikka (2012: 113) has noted in his media archaeological discussion of new media archives, this 'is the fate of media that become too effective in what they do. They vanish from view, do their job of mediating and leave the illusion that all there is is content passing through channels.' These common everyday cultural archives certainly seem to have become familiar and invisible media, and as a result the types of political issues that Bowker and Star point towards camouflage into the background. If we were being hasty, we might conclude that the fact that these new types of archives are open to content and ordering by 'the people' makes them democratic and empowering, or even that the collective effort behind them might be understood as a new solidarity or social collectiveness. But we need to be careful. These archives have changed, the hierarchies might be less visible but it does not mean that these hierarchies and structural systems of power do not reside within them. These are, after all, commercial spaces, at least in the large part. We might even want to consider the stratifications working to order people's right to tag or contribute content. Coolness, awkwardness, being an outsider, making judgements or comments or tags that receive negative reactions, and so on, might all be at play in the new formation of power within the archives. There are some complex questions yet to be considered in thinking through the power of these archives to order culture, and the power of metadata in these processes. It is important that self-organisation is not read as a flattening of all hierarchies of dominance and power.

Indeed, for Parikka (2012: 114) these archives have the power to create realities. His argument is that 'instead of narrative, the structural collections of data we call databases form new kinds of information reality enabled by computers' (Parikka, 2012: 114). We might sense here something close to Lyotard's (1979) arguments about the production of knowledge in an era of databases. In a detailed and compelling account of metadata and music, Jeremy Morris grounds this assertion in the practices of music consumption. Drawing upon examples from music metadata, Morris (2012: 10) claims that 'metadata are both descriptive and prescriptive'. He points out that the sorting of music might seem innocuous but that it 'also prescribes how users access and experience their music' and that 'metadata condition a user's experience of music', which, he notes, is increasingly the case with music based recommendation software such as Genius and Last.fm (Morris, 2012: 10; Beer, 2010). Morris' (2012: 14) point is that metadata contextualise digital data; he says that it 'takes the work of metadata to give digital music the context necessary for collecting it, using it, and interacting with it'. Without metadata, according to Morris, music is just data without context and without links (for more on the making of meaning around the collection of digital music files see Kibby, 2009).

Morris' work is helpful in grounding the notion that metadata prescribe a reality or an experience of culture, and his call to look at the 'micromaterials' of metadata is a useful starting point for a response. The case of music is also interesting because of how familiar the archives are that now organise musical consumption. Parikka argues that such archives and archiving, as familiar and embedded technologies, may be more distributed and variable than older archive forms. Yet the same questions of power still apply. Parikka (2012: 115) writes that:

> despite the distributed nature, one can argue that power still resides in the archive, which is now embedded in architectures of software, and the political economy of social media platforms whose revenue streams are based on the fact of individual everyday contributions through activity: Facebook, YouTube, Google, etc., gathering data on user patterns, preferences and consumer desires, for further evaluation, reuse and reselling purposes.

In order to understand the power relations around such new archives, it is Parikka's position that they need to be seen in the context of the political economy, as part of the flow and generation of capital, and as a part of capitalist structures. The form and content of such archives might be decentralised in form, but in order to understand the power differentials they need to be seen as decentralised within the broader political economy.

If we return though to the power of metadata and the ordering processes in these new cultural archives, then this also returns us to the discussion of memory. Clearly archives, as we have seen, are implicit in the production of individual and collective memory. We have to assume that the organisation of the archive is the organisation of memory. In the way that the content in the archive might shape memory, so too the way that the content is labelled, classified and made retrievable is powerful in fostering and maintaining such memory. The tagging processes and the algorithmic searching facilities (see also Chapter 4) often reveal what content is defined as most pertinent or relevant and thus shapes the 'memories' that are found or made. This sorting of the content also feeds into the reuse of data, not just in the routines of everyday life but also in the productive processes of remixing (Parikka, 2012: 134), of telling stories or revealing narratives (Abba, 2012) or even in secondary analysis (Geiger et al., 2010). Parikka notes that the issue of memory in these new archives is tied closely to their dynamic nature and how this dynamic content is maintained. He claims that:

> digital memory itself, on its socio-technical level, is vulnerable to limited duration and decay, and in need of constant maintenance. In social media culture, new forms of production, sharing and organizing content through, for example, the folksonomy of tagging practices presents again something far more dynamic than the traditional content and knowledge management procedures ... which relates to fundamental changes in cultural memory in software culture.
>
> (Parikka, 2012: 121)

For Parikka, the very dynamism of this content and its organisation pose questions for the power of these archives to shape memory. The sense of the instability of these archives, relative to older and more stable archives, opens questions about the ephemerality and retrievability of memories from within such a mass of changeable data and

metadata. It is interesting to note here a range of debates about how
the archive shapes the way that history is conducted and hence the
types of memories that might be extracted in this more formal story
telling (for a discussion of these issues see Geiger et al., 2010). We can
imagine that the form of the archive similarly translates to other
types of collective and individual memory making.

The power of the metadata in these archives in some ways is quite
simple. It shapes the culture we find, it shapes how we categorise it,
it shapes the distinctions we make in classification, and it also forms
a part of our own engagement with and contributions to cultural
ordering. Tagging is an embodiment of the classificatory imagination, it is how we find the material we are looking for, that is to
say it is how we navigate these cultural archives. Tagging is also
the practice of labelling or classifying the things around us, in this
case with globally disseminated classifications. Metadata tags order
culture. As a consequence these archives have at their centre a self-
organising classificatory system, one that might be open to abuse
but which tends to function surprisingly seamlessly for something so
decentralised. Perhaps the reason it functions in this way is because
the tagging process is actually a culmination of the shared cultural
grids, as Foucault put it, which inform the encoded eyes that come
to participate and use these cultural archives.

Conclusion

My overriding argument is that in order to understand culture we
need to develop a much clearer understanding of cultural archives
and the classificatory imagination. Within this, we need to understand the *infrastructures of participation*, but we also need to understand the *infrastructures of participative organisation*. This is to say that
in order to explore the significance of cultural data flows, we need
first to understand how these flows are organised. This is particularly
pressing given some of the changes I have outlined and the new types
of archives and classificatory processes that are now central to how
culture circulates. We cannot really hope to understand culture unless
we understand more about how it is being ordered and re-ordered in
the contemporary decentralised mediascape. Here I have suggested
that culture is now being archived and ordered through vast practices of tagging, which are now routine parts of cultural practice.

Tagging, as a form of metadata, has enabled the reworking of culture in a self-organising constellation of formats. How culture is encountered and understood is now, at least in part, a product of these processes. This type of classificatory imagination, shaping these cultural archives, now needs to be factored into accounts of culture and cultural consumption. Further to this we should also acknowledge that changes in the archiving of culture may also change the culture itself, as culture is increasingly designed or made for these archives. As Featherstone (2000: 180) has argued, '[s]hifts in archival technology do not merely change the form within which culture is recorded, but very much influence the future content of the archive by changing the conditions under which culture is produced and enacted'. There are echoes here then of Walter Benjamin's (1999a: 211–244) observations about the technologies of reproduction actually altering the production of culture. There is certainly a new politics of the cultural archive that shapes what culture is and how it might be experienced and studied.

The power of metadata is the power of the cultural encounter (see more on this in Chapter 4 on algorithms). As Bowker and Star and Foucault have made clear, systems of classification are deeply political and so are the archiving processes of which they are a part. They are central in shaping the cultural resources from which we might draw and thus shape memory and understanding. Archives are prescriptive. These archives both hold and create cultural data, allowing things to be found and creating new data traces as we do so. What is clear is that the hierarchies of cultural organisation have been challenged. The classificatory imagination has a more open playing field for re-classifying the culture it locates in these archives. The global dissemination of culture as digital data has gained much attention, but the global dissemination of the metadata that organises this data has received much less attention. As a result, the infrastructures of participation are becoming more visible, whilst the ordering powers of the infrastructures of participative organisation remain hidden. Here I have shown how such metadata, often in the form of tagging, are now both prevalent and powerful in shaping what culture is, how visible it is, and how it is accessed and understood. If, as some have suggested, we might want to 'scrape' data from these archives, then we need to be clearer about what they are, what they contain and how they are organised. Only then can we hope to fully understand what might be obtained from such data.

Structurally speaking the gatekeepers of these archives are now the users, they can add content and decide how to order it. This is an important change. Perhaps the area for further development now, is to explore how these decentralised plural forms of classifications compete and imbricate with other more centralised and formal classifications within and across different types of archives (for a typology of archives in popular culture, see Beer and Burrows, 2013). The contentious classifications will maintain their visibility, as Bowker and Star suggested, but perhaps we now need to understand how archiving is central to culture and how different systems of classification lead to different understandings of cultural forms and different cultural encounters. Bowker and Star's (1999: 324–325) suggestion that we uncover these processes by taking three steps is pertinent here: 'recognizing the balancing act of classifying', 'rendering voice retrievable' and 'being sensitive to exclusions'. This is important in terms of the everyday politics, the 'practical ontology' (Bowker and Star, 1999), of cultural consumption. What we consume is very likely to shape our view of the world. It is also important for us now to see the reshaping of culture beyond well-practiced lines of class, community and subculture, and towards the new vistas that these archives open. This would be to consider how social connections are re-forged in these acts of communal organisation and negotiation. This will be quite a challenge. To move further in this direction, the following chapter attempts to understand how such cultural encounters might also be shaped by the non-human agents that are software algorithms.

4
Algorithms: Shaping Tastes and Manipulating the Circulations of Popular Culture

Introduction: Measuring and predicting cultural tastes

In 2006 Netflix, a subscription based online film and TV provider, ran a competition inviting people to help to improve their 'most valued...assets' their 'recommendation system' (Netflix, 2012). This was described as a 'machine learning and data mining competition for movie rating prediction'. A $1m prize was available to 'whoever improved the accuracy of [the] existing system...by 10%' (Netflix, 2012). The aim of this competition they say, in true 'knowing capitalism' (Thrift, 2005) style, was to 'find new ways to improve the recommendations we provide to our members, which is a key part of our business'. The aim then was to find a way of suggesting films to customers that would more closely suit their tastes and to make better predictions about what they were likely to want to watch. The aim was to reduce the error level of such prediction from the root mean squared error of 0.9525 to 0.8572 or less. What is interesting here is not only the systems of prediction that are central to this form of cultural consumption, with films and TV being suggested to us by the devices, but also that the prediction of cultural taste can be metricised. Taste predictions can be turned into a number that represents the accuracy of the prediction. In many ways this example is a microcosm of the processes and underlying cultural infrastructures that are indicative of the arguments of this book. Here data is used to hone the predictive skills of the software and to make ever more powerful recommendations to the users. In other words, this is a kind of enactment through method (Law, 2004). This is predictive software shaping everyday cultural encounters in ways that are turned into numbers so that they can themselves be measured and altered. The implicit claim in the Netflix competition is that the influence of algorithms on cultural taste is measurable.

In the case of the Netflix competition, a team of developers won the competition with an 8.43 per cent improvement in the accuracy of the predictive recommendation system – we are told that it took 2000 hours of work to put together the combination of 107 algorithms (Netflix, 2012). This material on the Netflix competition reveals how central the accuracy of the recommendation system is to such organisations, with the company working to increase the accuracy of the predictive capacity of their service and to base this around the personalisation of the individual profiles. What this also reveals more broadly, and if we generalise from this one instance, is that contemporary popular culture is being defined and shaped by these underlying collections of algorithms. In short, if we think across all such cultural consumption we can only imagine the density of algorithmic processes and the complex ways that they are now a part of the ordering, structuring and sorting of culture.

The chapter begins with some reflections on what algorithms are and how they have become such powerful social actors. This is then followed with a section that locates the power dynamics of algorithms and how it is that they come to enact parts of the social world. These first sections provide a broad socio-technological backdrop to the study of algorithms; in the following sections the chapter draws upon these founding ideas to move towards the incorporation of algorithms into cultural analysis, first by thinking about algorithms and culture and then by focusing more centrally upon the shaping of cultural encounters and cultural taste. The chapter closes with some conclusions about how this agenda might be developed and how further work might incorporate algorithmic power. This concluding section is also used to think about how the discussion of algorithms might challenge our understanding of how culture works, how it is located and how it circulates through friendship groups and taste communities. One observation is that if cultural taste is central to an understanding of class and social mobility, then we might need to think about how such relations work where algorithms become active in such hierarchies.

Algorithms . . . a return to software sorting

Adrian Mackenzie (2006: 43) notes that '[s]oftware cannot do with-out, according to computer science, algorithms and data structures'. Algorithms are the organising structures in the software that, we are told, are sinking into everyday life (see Chapter 2). As the computer scientist Herbert S. Wilf describes, an 'algorithm is a method for solv-ing a class of problems on a computer' (Wilf, 2002: 1). Or as Cormen et al. (1990: 1) explain, 'an algorithm is any well-defined compu-tational procedure that takes some value, or set of values, as input and produces some value, or set of values, as output'. Baase and Van Gelder (2000: 2) add that to 'say a problem is algorithmically solv-able means, informally, that a computer program can be written that will produce the correct answer for any input . . . Much of the early work in this field, was on describing or characterizing those prob-lems that could be solved algorithmically and on exhibiting some problems that could not be.' The concern for a social scientist might be this notion of a correct outcome and how this might be measured. Alongside this, of course, we might wonder if the output of the algo-rithm becomes a self-fulfilling outcome, as it comes to act on the world rather than being neutral within it.

So, algorithms are the problem-solving devices in software and code. These types of problems range in form, but many begin with the need to sort data into categories and types. There are many algorithms for this type of classification and sorting work (Cormen et al., 1990: 3–4; and for an overview of types of sorting algorithm see Baase and Van Gelder, 2000: 150–221). In an introductory guide Jeff Edmonds explains the differences, '[a]n *algorithm* is a step-by-step procedure which, starting with an input instance, produces a suitable output . . . In contrast, *code* is an implementation of an algo-rithm that can be executed by a computer. *Pseudocode* lies between these two' (Edmonds, 2008: 1). Again, algorithms represent the order-ing structures in code. Writing in the late 1980s, Robert Sedgewick (1988: 4) warns though that even simple algorithms can lead to 'complicated data structures' (see also Cormen et al., 1990: 6).

In a recently published book titled *9 Algorithms That Changed the Future* (2012) the computer scientist John MacCormick outlines nine types of algorithm that have been most influential, and in the process he reveals how central algorithms are to contemporary society. In one chapter, for instance, he outlines the algorithms that are used in the compression of files, such as MP3 and the like, which we have heard so much about in music consumption. Similarly JPEG compression algorithms have compressed visual images for circulation. MacCormick also describes the algorithms behind the indexing that allows search engines to work, the ranking system on Google that prioritises the most relevant materials when we are searching, the algorithms that enable content to be communicated securely as well as descriptions of the algorithms used in pattern recognition, for consistency in databases like Facebook and for the correction of errors in everyday internet use. Rather than explore the details of these algorithms, which MacCormick does with some granularity, we can instead reflect upon how the general content of the book intimates towards the vast presence of algorithms in contemporary everyday practices and routines, and how algorithms are now a deeply embedded part of the production, dissemination and consumption of culture. As an example, we might reflect on how powerful something like Google's PageRank is in shaping what we encounter when we search. By making judgements about relevance this algorithm, by prioritising content, is shaping our encounters with information (for a description of how this algorithm makes judgements based on hyperlinks and the perceived authority of these links see MacCormick, 2012: 24–37; see also Mager, 2012).

Before we reflect on this further, we can think for a moment about what these algorithms actually are and how they underpin these processes and systems. MacCormick (2012: 3), attempting to introduce algorithms to a broad non-specialist audience, suggests that 'an algorithm is a precise recipe that specifies the exact sequence of steps required to solve a problem'. Clearly this is a very basic working definition, but it takes the algorithm to the core of its function. MacCormick works with the example of a simple algorithm that we all learn at school, the algorithm for adding together two large numbers. MacCormick (2012: 3) describes this process:

> The algorithm involves a sequence of steps that starts off something like this: 'First, add the final digits of the two numbers together, write down the final digit of the result, and carry any other digits to the next column on the left; second, add the digits

in the next column together, add on any carried digits from the previous column...' – and so on.

This, MacCormick points out, is a basic algorithm. A series of steps or points in the 'recipe' that lead directly to the outcome. These basics steps are rigid and prescriptive and lead to an intended output. As he adds:

> One of the key features of an algorithm: each of the steps must be absolutely precise, requiring no human intuition or guesswork. That way, each of the purely mechanical steps can be programmed into a computer. Another important feature of an algorithm is that it always works, no matter what the inputs.
>
> (MacCormick, 2012: 3)

Here MacCormick refers back to the addition algorithm to suggest that whatever numbers you put into the algorithm, it will always work. In very basic terms then an algorithm solves a problem – although some problems fall into the undecidables and cannot be addressed in this way (MacCormick, 2012: 174–198). But the key point for MacCormick (2012: 4), who of course is a computer scientist and is looking at algorithms for their problem solving potential rather than their social and cultural affect, is that 'computers need to be programmed with very precise instructions... before we can get a computer to solve a particular problem for us, we need to develop an algorithm for that problem'. This is a very functional vision of algorithms as the underlying sequences or steps of computation that lead to the resolution of specific problems. This is useful in providing a sense of the basic types of functions of algorithms and the hidden depths of algorithmic processes in everyday life (Beer, 2009b). To gain a greater understanding of these in everyday processes, it is worth thinking of these algorithms as an integrated part of the social world. To do this we need not lose sight of the material functioning of algorithms but, as with other technologies, it is helpful to begin to see them as an embedded part of social processes that are enacted in various settings (Hayles, 1999). Adrian Mackenize (2006: 43) points out that algorithms 'carry, fold, frame and redistribute actions into different environments'. Mackenzie's argument is that because of this, and because software is central to the new connectivities that flow into the environment, so the 'analysis of the mode of existence of algorithms becomes critical' (Mackenzie, 2006: 43). Mackenzie (2006) is arguing here for a social analysis of algorithms that understands how they 'animate', 'order' and 'sequence' the social world. To give an example, in his later collaborative work on code, Mackenzie suggests that crises, be they financial, ecological, cultural or psychological, commonly flow into everyday life through code. This occurs, according to Mackenzie and Vurdubakis (2011: 4), because code is so deeply embedded in the everyday and because these crises are inscribed in the code itself.

Algorithms and the making of the social world... or why it is that algorithms matter

So what then might a critical and socially embedded approach to algorithms look like? It is fair to say that outside of a few exceptions, many of which I will discuss in this chapter, there has been very little acknowledgement in the social sciences and humanities of the role of algorithms. As the above indicates, Mackenzie's (2006) provocative study of software is a good place to start. Using examples from 'bioinformatics', Mackenzie begins to set out an agenda for the development of a more social understanding of algorithms and their functions. He suggests the following as a starting point: a 'critical analysis of algorithms would start by recognizing that the expectation that things will be in place is historically and socially specific. Order and sequence are the result of much work' (Mackenzie, 2006: 44). The central issue in the study of algorithms for Mackenzie is the issue of ordering. Algorithms order, he claims, and they have the capacity to make this ordering look natural, unequivocal and definitive. The algorithms here are not necessarily creating a new order, this is not an entirely new 'cyberbole' (Woolgar, 2002) based upon rules made by machines, but may be part of the continuation of historical ordering processes played out through the boundaries they create in the software and its outputs. This, Mackenzie claims, has powerful social implications. As he describes:

> An algorithm selects and reinforces one ordering at the expense of others. Agency, therefore, is by definition contested in and through algorithms. They affect what can be said and done...It both naturalizes certain orders and animates certain

movements. An algorithm naturalizes who does what to whom by subsuming existing patterns and orderings of cognition, communication and movement.

(Mackenzie, 2006: 44)

The scale of the social influence of algorithms, for Mackenzie, starts to become clear here. This is a vision of algorithms as powerful social actors that shape possibilities and limit agency, suggesting the far reaching effects of algorithms in the social world. Algorithms here become a kind of invisible structural force that plays through into everyday life in various ways. This is similar to what Scott Lash (2007; Beer, 2009b) has described elsewhere as 'power through the algorithm'. For Lash these algorithms are creating or reinforcing sets of social rules that may be understood as a new form of power. As Galloway (2011: 95) also adds, 'the point of power today is not in the image', rather he claims that the 'point of power today resides in networks, computers, algorithms, information and data'. With algorithms, Galloway argues, being an 'unrepresentable' force.

Lash, with echoes of Mackenzie's position, says that '[c]omputer scientists understand algorithms in terms of "rules" ... but these rules are far different from the sorts of rules that human scientists have dealt with over the decades' (Lash, 2007: 70). Lash suggests that what has changed is that where we once might have focused an understanding of power and regulation upon 'constitutive' and 'regulative' rules, now, 'in a society of pervasive media and ubiquitous coding, at stake is a third type of rule, algorithmic, *generative* rules' (Lash, 2007: 71). This is a new form of power, according to Lash, a post-hegemonic power that operates from the inside rather than being about the dominant acting on the dominated through ideology. Lash explains that these:

> Generative rules are, as it were, virtuals, that generate a whole variety of actuals. They are compressed and hidden and we do not encounter them in the way that we encounter constitutive and regulative rules. Yet this third type of generative rule is more and more pervasive in our social and cultural life of post-hegemonic order. They do not merely open up opportunity for invention, however. They are also pathways through which capitalist power works.
>
> (Lash, 2007: 71)

In other words, for Lash, algorithms create realities, they constitute the social world in different ways and they present us with limitations and boundaries that we then live by. We begin to see straight away, however we might feel about Lash and Mackenzie's provocative positions, that algorithms could well be operating to create or maintain rules and orders without really being noticed. They operate, as Thrift (2005) has put it, in the 'technological unconscious' – indeed, the lack of awareness or visibility of these powerful algorithmic processes has been something of an area of consensus (as well as Thrift, 2005; see also Graham, 2005, and Hayles, 2006).

The above suggests that algorithms need to be understood as a part of the social world in order to understand the power they have to shape everyday life. Before moving to look at the implications of algorithms for popular culture, let us turn now to a range of literature that deals with the social implications of the increasing embeddedness of algorithms in social processes. By turning to this literature we can then begin to develop a conceptual vocabulary and approach for thinking in more detail about algorithms in culture.

A common theme, reflected in Mackenzie's central argument, concerns the relations between algorithms and agency, or the contestation of agency, to be more specific, and how these become 'invisible' as they 'increasingly pattern and coordinate everyday life' (Mackenzie, 2006: 45). Mackenzie (2006: 65) concludes that:

> The contestation of agency here concerns how action is both naturalized and animated, made to seem ordinary and extraordinary. Here the contestation of agency pivots on the composite, concatenated patterns and orderings that algorithms condense ... [no] actual algorithm [is] unattached from the orderings, positionings and sequencings that increasingly weave software into environments.

As software become part of environments so their ordering and sequencing become natural parts of the social world. Thus agency is challenged or contested by these naturalised boundaries, according to Mackenzie, in often unseen and invisible ways. The ordering powers of algorithms are far reaching and are highly prescriptive as they come, via the embedded software, to constitute, shape and order everyday life.

In order to attempt to unpick or understand the ordering power of algorithms and their relations with human agency, Mackenzie, again using bioinformatics as the case study, suggests three 'general implications' that can be explored. It is worth outlining these as a reference point for the discussion of the types of implications and conceptualisations we see emerging in the other writings on algorithms.

First, Mackenzie outlines the abstract nature of algorithms and how their abstractions are translated into sequences, orders and timings. Algorithms may be abstract but they enact material processes. Indeed, what he describes as 'algorithmic time' is an important aspect of this for Mackenzie. He contends that algorithms 'do not simply speed up computation; they institute a composite time and space in which existing orderings and sequences are both preserved and reconfigured' (Mackenzie, 2006: 64). Orders and sequences then, which may be the product of existing tendencies, shift on to the time-scales of the algorithm as it works through its sequences with its allocated computational power. As such the algorithm translates its ordering into the pace or speed of these everyday processes. We come to live, as it were, in 'algorithmic time'.

Second, Mackenzie highlights the 'entwined framings at work in algorithms'. Here the claim is that every 'abstraction is relative to a concrete framing...Considerations of computational space and time can be found at each level of abstraction in algorithmic design, ranging from theoretical estimations of algorithmic complexity...to optimizations in the flow of code that individual programmers implement in well-known algorithms' (Mackenzie, 2006: 64). For a specific example of this kind of framing Jussi Parikka has described how nature, and particularly insects and swarms, have acted as the model by which software and algorithms have been designed, with the replication of nature's 'perfect machine' being the objective (Parikka, 2010: 145–168; see also Thacker, 2007; and for more on nature, genetics and algorithms see DeLanda, 2011: 48–78). This then is about the social embeddedness of algorithms. It is about seeing algorithms not as abstract lines of code but to see them in their social settings as they become a part of routines and processes. This understanding of the framing of algorithms is concerned with how algorithms allow 'software to flow into everyday life' (Mackenzie, 2006: 64). This framing is both the way in which the software is imagined in the design stages and how this then feeds into practice. Elsewhere, along similar lines, Kitchin and Dodge say that '[d]evelopers often unconsciously place a particular philosophical frame on the world that renders it amenable to the work of code and algorithms, thus realizing a specific system of thought to address a particular relational problem' (Kitchin and Dodge, 2011: 247). So these social frames are abstractions that enable the software to become part of everyday processes, bringing with them broader social and historical frameworks based upon influences such as nature, biography and even moral frameworks (see Lyon in Kitchin and Dodge, 2011: 104). Algorithms solve problems in particular ways.

Third, Mackenzie's (2006: 64–65) final implications are based on the 'points of attachment between algorithms and other movements and space'. This is about the ways in which the framing of the software become a part of the context in which they operate. Here the algorithm becomes a part of complex social processes, rather than just having implications for the immediate process of which it is a part. Mackenzie (2006: 65) argues that:

> Algorithms are not neutral formal procedures. In algorithms that predict or correlate sequences of events in living systems, the treatment of living systems as algorithms in process is enmeshed with the broader promises of bioinformatics as source of scientific knowledge and economic value... Algorithms themselves are animated: they induce movement between inputs and outputs, and are themselves caught up in diagonal movements between biological knowledge and property value, movements characteristic of the new media biotechnology economy.

Algorithms, in this working, can no longer be seen as neutral problem-solving devices. This final set of implications is concerned with seeing the vast emergence of affect associated with algorithmic processes. As such it is necessary to view algorithms both as a part of the social fabric and as a part of a network of interrelated social processes. Algorithms are both a product and a part of these increasingly software dense environments.

In Mackenzie's writings we have some useful guide points that emerge from this early work on algorithms in the bioinformatics sector. The general guidelines he provides are helpful in shifting away from a neutral and computer scientific vision of algorithms and towards a vision of algorithms as being deeply embedded in social processes. Of course, the central issue revolves around the relations between algorithms and agency.

Algorithms and agency

As discussed in Chapter 2, Kitchin and Dodge (2011) have influentially argued that software is now central to social functioning (we can locate similar arguments across a range of other articles, most notably Crang and Graham, 2007). What they describe as 'code/space' (see Chapter 2) is riddled with algorithms. Kitchin and Dodge provide a detailed account of how algorithms have become a defining part of various aspects of the social world from air flight to the home. They point out that:

> Software has, at a fundamental level, an ontological power, it is able to realize whole systems of thought (algorithms and capta) with respect to specific domains. For example, consider the influence of formalizing and coding how money is represented and transacted and thus how the banking system is organized and works.
>
> (Kitchin and Dodge, 2011: 26)

The point here is that software algorithms, as has already been suggested, are deeply embedded in a range of social spheres. It should be added that others have acknowledged the power of algorithms in the banking sector (see Gane, 2012b: 66–70). This work has included an account of how algorithmic trading occurs in the financial sector, making trading decisions through the 'Volume Weighted Average Price' or 'VWAP algorithm' (Lenglet, 2011: 49), and the way that codings might end up being 'misaligned' from codes of conduct (Lenglet, 2011: 61). Again, this work describes the way that algorithmic agency intervenes in or bypasses human discretion.

It is notable that Kitchin and Dodge talk here of algorithms as systems of thought. The software, which is becoming incorporated into various spheres, they argue, has ontological powers in that it realises these systems of thought in different social settings. Again, this is a parallel argument to Lash and Mackenzie, in that we see the way that algorithms have an ordering power that frames the possibilities of action and understanding. The point being that algorithms, as an ordering mechanism of code, are a part of the 'terrain on which decisions concerning chance, pattern, order, values, time, otherness, nature and culture are enacted' (Mackenzie and Vurdubakis, 2011: 4).

By way of illustration of the relations between algorithms, capta – which are selected units of measurement – and 'the world', Kitchin and Dodge turn to weather and climate change modelling. They describe this in the following terms:

> Here, knowledge about the world is translated and formalised into capta structures and algorithms that are then converted into sets of computational instructions that when applied to climate measurements express a particular story. Gramelsberger expresses this as 'Theory = Mathematics = Code = Story.' Our understanding of weather forecasting and climate models are almost entirely driven by these computational models, which have been refined over time in a recursive fashion in response to how these models have performed, and which are used to theorise, simulate and predict weather patterns...In turn, the models underpin policy arguments concerning climate change and have real effects concerning individual and institutional responses to measured and predicted change...the models analyze the world and the world responds to the models.
>
> (Kitchin and Dodge, 2011: 30)

A similar account then to the opening vignette on the Netflix predictive algorithm. These are recursive processes with algorithms being measured, honed and refined to suit the systems of measurement and the story they fit within – 'the models analyze the world and the world responds to the models'. We can return to the issues of recursivity and ordering in understanding the social power of algorithms, but let us stick for the moment with the issue of agency that still underpins this unfolding power of algorithms in everyday processes. In the above passage from Kitchin and Dodge, we see that knowledge and decision-making in the policy setting is informed by algorithmic processes. As such the agency of the algorithm feeds directly into the agency of 'the committee' – something that would have proven to provide a nice extension to the arguments about the committee and bureaucratic functioning in the academy made by C. Wright Mills (1959). A clear instance then of data feeding back into decision-making through algorithmic processes.

For Mike Crang and Stephen Graham (2007), we can think of the relations between algorithms and agency in spatial terms as enveloped in the 'sentient city', wrapped up as it is in 'ubiquitous computing' and 'ambient intelligence'. 'Urban ubiquitous computing systems', they argue, 'entwine people, place and software in complex ways. Software algorithms code people, places and their data in interrelated systems that are then used to profile and drive decision making systems. This raises a key question: What happens when the processing and not just the data is embedded in the everyday environment?' (Crang and Graham, 2007: 792). The result is that such processes embed themselves and become a part of the architecture of everyday life. As such a 'wide range of technologies deploying algorithmic calculation, tracking and data mining are being deployed to reconfigure passport systems, borders, even public transport transactions, based on the biometric tracking of identities' (Crang and Graham, 2007: 802). As things stand we can only begin to imagine the power of such processes and the types of consequences they might have. As Jordan Crandall (2010: 69) describes:

> The history of tracking is rooted in the figure of the surveilant – the observational expert, stationed at the monitors of policing, military and intelligence agencies, interpreting movements on images maps or screens. Yet tracking practices have developed in ways that complicate this centralization of human agency. They have come to rely, increasingly, on algorithmic procedures and automated systems, and they have been incorporated into distributed network environments – augmented by new sensing and locationing technologies and embedded into mobile devices, buildings, cars and urban infrastructures.

Again in this account of tracking and surveillance, the expert judgement of the human agent is bypassed by algorithmic systems of judgement. Crandall's account envisions this expert as now being a part of an infrastructure that makes the decisions. This, he claims, complicates the centrality of human agency in such processes of risk assessment. It is not, for Crandall, that human agency is lost altogether, but rather that it becomes a part of these lively infrastructures.

In order to flesh this vision out we can take the work of Louise Amoore as an example. Her empirical work has shown how in the control of national borders, border guards 'defer security decisions into algorithmic calculation' (Amoore, 2009b: 63). Or, as she describes further elsewhere, the 'data derivative comes into being from an amalgam of disaggregated data – reaggregated via mobile algorithm-based association rules and visualised in "real time" as risk map, score or colour-coded flag' (Amoore, 2011: 27). These, Amoore (2011: 27) argues, 'go on to live and act in the world'. Data derivatives, Amoore notes, become the basis from which predictions are made about potential behaviours or actions – and thus understanding their origins and their part in these systems is crucial in revealing the underlying logics and politics of these decision-making processes. The crucial point here is that such decisions then become the product of algorithmic agency, and various types of data resources, rather than being based upon human discretion. These data resources, as they feed into data derivatives, can be 'fragmented' and are often being used in inferential practices far from their intended uses (Amoore, 2011: 28). As Amoore (2011: 28) adds, 'the data derivative is not centred on who we are, nor even on what our data says about us, but on what can be imagined and inferred about who we might be – on our very proclivities and potentialities'. In this case the decisions about who or what constitutes a risk are made by the processing and sorting powers of algorithms. The data and the means of analysis are inherent in these infrastructures. As Crang and Graham put it, these systems are used 'to call upon memories, via databases recording the history of movements and associations of things, activities and people, and anticipate, so that threatening and "abnormal" behaviours and emergences can be detected and dealt with before the point of terrorist or insurgent attack' (Crang and Graham, 2007: 801–802). These are important politically orientated decisions that are made through the data and analytical functions of the 'sentient city'. As Crandall (2010: 83) notes in an article about tracking and algorithms, such tracking systems:

> can adapt to changes in the observed environment 'on its own', detecting, tracking and classifying abnormal behaviour that was

not previously defined or anticipated – activity that might be deemed high-risk or potentially violent...Since they occur with little or no human involvement, minimizing the need for human intervention or dispensing with it altogether, such activities are often understood to occur 'automatically' or 'autonomously'. In this way the algorithm is dehumanized.

We need not necessarily assume that this algorithmic agency is accurate, the mere fact that it exists and that it reshapes decision-making is important. Here it is clear that algorithms are having, as Crandall claims, a 'dehumanizing' affect on those being judged and on those making the judgements. There are a set of contrasting norms that individuals are judged against by these systems without human discretion intervening or altering decisions. Crandall argues though that human input into the crafting of algorithms and their decision-making processes complicates matters (the new forms of agency that emerge or are borrowed by algorithms have been discussed in terms of the 'encoding of human' agency by Introna, 2011: 122–130). Crandall contends that the rise of such processes is not a movement into a new machine age but is rather the development of a set of circumstances within which different types of agency combine (Crandall, 2010: 83–84). This is illustrated by the descriptions of the computer scientist Robert Sedgewick (1988: 81), who, from early in the development of computer algorithms, pointed out that algorithms 'rarely exist in a vacuum ... [p]roper algorithm design involves putting some thought into the potential impact of design decisions on implementations, and proper applications of programming involves putting some thought into performance properties of the basic methods used'. The design of the algorithm then is very much a product of the understanding of the outcomes it is likely to create and is therefore shaped by the judgement of the designer.

This though is not just about the moments in which such big decisions are made, it is also about the way that these decisions are informed by contextualising data of various types. This background information is central in enabling the decision-making processes to occur. As Crang and Graham note, '[c]rucial here is the adaptation of the commercial practices of "data mining" or "predictive analytics" where algorithms are developed to look for patterns in the swathes of captured data, identify or profile behaviours or characteristics deemed to be "unusual" or "abnormal"' (Crang and Graham, 2007: 803). And as we now know, the depth of information about us is only growing and spreading across most areas of everyday life, including music and popular culture (Beer, 2010). The result is that there is a plethora of information about us that can be used as a resource to inform algorithmic agency. Stephen Graham, summarising such processes of 'software sorting', directly raises such questions of agency when he points out that 'computer algorithms are being used at the interface of databases and telecommunications networks to allocate different levels of service to different users on an increasingly automated basis' (Graham, 2004c: 325). Indeed, it has been argued that it is the sorting and categorising of things and people that is the real power of algorithms and, in this simple act of 'data differentiation', is where they have the most social consequence (Cheney-Lippold, 2011: 166–172). The point here is that, thanks to some detailed empirical work, some of which I will discuss in more detail below, there are now moments where we might begin to see the agentic power of algorithms as they come to take decisions out of people's hands. The consequence appears to be the meshing of agency in these environments. This work has focused on some key areas, particularly in political geography, but the net can be opened to imagine that the same meshing of agency is emerging, or is even already established, across a range of sectors, with algorithms shaping or making decisions and thus becoming active agents that constitute and shape as well as maintain and facilitate.

Algorithms and recursivity: The iterative dimensions of social life

There are types of algorithms that are specifically designed to facilitate recursive processes. Thus there are engineered forms of recursivity that are part of these software structures. Jeff Edmonds (2008: 2) points out that:

> Most algorithms are best described as being either *iterative* or *recursive*. An iterative algorithm (...) takes one step at a time ... A recursive algorithm (...) breaks its instances into smaller instances, which it gets a *friend* to solve, and then combines their solutions into one of its own ... Recursive backtracking algorithms (...) try things and, if they don't work, backtrack and try something else.

These algorithms are either based upon linear stages, or they weave together circulations of algorithmic processes to produce overarching outcomes – and this is before we enter into the functionality of other types of algorithms such as 'greedy algorithms' (Edmonds, 2008: 225–250), 'dynamic programming algorithms' (Edmonds, 2008: 267–292), 'searching algorithms' (Sedgewick, 1988: 193–259), 'sorting algorithms' (Sedgewick, 1988: 93–177), 'graph algorithms' (Cormen et al., 1990: 463–465), 'parallel algorithms' (Baase and Van Gelder, 2000: 612–647) and so on. Underpinning these are a history of algorithm development in mathematics and some well-established 'classic algorithms' (Baase and Van Gelder, 2000: 2). Some algorithms are specifically designed to draw together looped outcomes that bring the decision-making processes back in on themselves to form continual loops. These are self-referential systems.

In a chapter on 'recursive algorithms' Herbert S. Wilf (2002: 49–98) outlines the central features of their functioning. Wilf (2002: 50) points out that the 'hallmark of a recursive procedure is that it *calls itself*'. These algorithms *call themselves*, that is to say that they feed into their own functioning (for more on algorithms calling themselves, see also Sedgewick, 1988: 51). They loop back into themselves in their own processes, thus forming a circular system or looped systems. 'Recursion trees' are then used to analyse the outputs and structures of these recursive algorithms and to measure the 'cost', in terms of 'running time, number of key comparisons and other measures' (Baase and Van Gelder, 2000: 134). Sedgewick (1988: 51) adds that often a 'termination condition' is required to allow the program to stop calling itself when necessary and to prevent it from never stopping. Wilf (2002), writing a decade or so ago, indicates some excitement and awe about the potential of such recursive algorithms. He continues by saying that 'many methods of great power are being formulated recursively, methods which, in many cases, might not have been developed if recursion were not readily available as a practical programming tool' (Wilf, 2002: 50). Wilf appears to be outlining the power of the new potential possibilities of recursive algorithms; we can quickly imagine how such processes have now sunk into the ordinary functioning of software code in the decade or so since his book was published.

Clearly then there are recursive structures built into the infrastructures of new media that have now become mainstream in everyday life. It is worth reflecting back here on how this type of recursion might have implications for our earlier discussion of agency. There is already some suggestion in this chapter that social models and desired outcomes become a part of algorithmic design and functioning, which suggests that algorithms are by no means free of human agency. This issue resurfaces when considering recursive algorithms. For instance, according to Wilf (2002: 50), 'there is a bit of art involved in choosing the list of variables on which a recursive procedure operates' (Wilf, 2002: 50). The processes of recursivity are not neutral or entirely machinic, rather they are shaped by the choices made and by the 'art' of the designer. Again we find the meshing of forms of agency, not just in the design of the algorithm but also in the types of data resources the algorithm draws from in solving the problem.

We have already seen from Kitchin and Dodge's discussion of weather and climate change prediction that algorithms are not fixed but are part of recursive social modelling – this is also suggested by the Netflix example and in Mackenzie's discussion of framing. Algorithms are themselves folded into circulations of knowledge as they both reflect knowledge about the world and as their performance is measured and refined to designed outcomes. However arbitrary, strange or inaccurate the systems of measurement that define this refining of the algorithm might be, they still have concrete outcomes. The systems for measuring the performance of algorithms and refining their functions are 'virtuals' that become 'actuals' (Lash, 2007) – see again the Netflix example. In these recursive processes we find the agency of algorithms again rubs up against the agency of human actors.

Echoing Mackenzie's accounts of how algorithms are abstracted theories about the world, Kitchin and Dodge (2011: 41) argue that:

> One of the effects of abstracting the world into software algorithms and data models, and rendering aspects of the world as capta, which are then used as the basis for software to do work in the world, is that the world starts to structure itself in the image of the capta and the code – a self-fulfilling, recursive relationship develops.

This is a crucial observation. It is acknowledgement of the way that these algorithms, and the systems of measurement that feed into them, have the capacity to become active in shaping and constituting social life. If we think of Netflix again, then it is likely that the films that are recommended to you by these algorithmic processes are likely to become the films you watch or that you are likely to want to watch. These are complex social processes that are impossible to unpick and to separate out, but fit more closely with discussions of emergence in complexity theory (Urry, 2003). Whatever the conceptual backdrop used to clarify these processes, it becomes clear that algorithms are an integrated and irretractable part of everyday social processes. They have the potential to become a reality and to reinforce, maintain or even reshape visions of the social world, knowledge and encounters with information. But they do not stand-alone; they are involved in a complex mix of knowledge and framings of the world. They simultaneously then become actors and shape what that knowledge of the world is. It is for this reason that Kitchin and Dodge (2011: 43) suggest the following formulation:

> Code is an expression of how computation both capture the world within a system of thought (as algorithms and structures of capta) and a set of instructions that tell digital hardware and communication networks how to act in the world. For us, software needs to be theorized as both a contingent product of the world and a relational producer of the world.

This is an important observation about the recursive nature of algorithmic processes. They are formed out of knowledge about the world and measured against that knowledge for their performance, but at the same time they are 'actants' in that world, shaping what it is and how it functions. This is probably one of the must powerful yet under acknowledged points of observation in recent times. Cultural analysis for example, has yet to engage with this observation or with the implications it alludes to for the changing ontology (or doing) of culture.

This changing ontology, as Scott Lash (2006 and 2007) has also described, is defined by the increasing possibilities for data to 'find us'. This is where data folds back into the social world and begins to not just capture it but also to 'constitute it' (Lash, 2007). They make the world. We do not need necessarily to search for things, because they come to us. Here algorithms are involved in recursive processes as they shape what data flows where and to whom. Algorithms define what 'finds us', and so have a powerful place in the circulations of data and how these are filtered and directed. This is a key new form of power, according to Lash (2007), which he describes as being post-hegemonic. By post-hegemonic he means that it is a form of power that does not act on someone from above, through ideology, but rather it is an immanent form of power that acts within lives by shaping and constituting lifeworlds (for an overview of this argument, see Beer 2009b). For Adrian Mackenzie these processes of data finding-us are part of what he calls the 'performativity' of code and the 'performativity of circulation'. Mackenzie notes, for example, that:

> As culture becomes 'operational', or as information technologies become more cultural, that is, as they merge into wider circulatory practices of ordering and coding, of representing and regulating differences in some ways and not others, erstwhile infrastructural things like operating systems, protocols, algorithms and code figure as singularities.
>
> (Mackenzie, 2005: 74)

Again we see here that the performance of circulation that occurs, the circulations that define what 'finds us', are the product of such systems. Mackenzie's point is that such systems have merged into wider cultural process and have become a part of how culture is ordered and organised. These infrastructures, for Mackenzie and Lash, have become part of the everyday, they have become cultural themselves as well as becoming a part of how culture is organised and consumed. This incorporation into the everyday combines with the ability to shape the things that find us and to constitute space and cultural experience. For Lash and Mackenzie these algorithms are powerful devices. This power comes from the way that they are implicit in the recursive and iterative processes that define everyday life.

Finally, to add an additional layer to these recursive and iterative processes we might also imagine that these algorithms are powerful not just in shaping encounters but also in shaping behaviour. If data are able to find us, then we might imagine that behaviours might be shaped by these data. Here behaviours and action might become a product of attempts to play with outcomes, to predict algorithmic processes and to try to shape the way that these algorithmic circulations occur. In a piece on what she describes as the ideology of algorithms Astrid Mager talks of the way that 'website providers not only provide content and links to search engines use to index the web, but also deliberately please search engines by designing their sites according to search algorithms' (Mager, 2012: 777). These she describes as being examples of how algorithmic processes also become a part of social action, based that is not just upon what they do but on how individuals and organisations respond to what they do – or to what they think they might do. But the iteration does not end there. Rather, in response, these 'marketing strategies alter search algorithms by forcing engineers to "tweak" the algorithm to maintain the quality of search results' (Mager, 2012: 777). The algorithms are then shaped and reshaped in response to these games and to try to prevent certain forms of behaviours, or to guide the processes towards more specified desired outcomes. Here we see that the algorithms themselves, which are affording these recursive cultural processes of data circulation, are a part of these iterative processes as they are redesigned and rewritten in response to these feedback loops. As Mager claims, there is an 'engineering-driven logic underlying the construction of search algorithms' (Mager, 2012: 775). They are far from fixed properties, but in defining what finds us, they are in turn rewritten, as we saw with the Netflix example, in response to the way that the circulations play out. Here then we have complex layers of recursive and iterative processes each implicating the other in various ways. This we can begin to imagine sits quite nicely with accounts of emergence, chaos and social complexity (Urry, 2003).

Algorithms, ordering and control

The above sections have briefly discussed how algorithms have come to have implications for agency and for defining recursive cultural flows and circulations. With this as a background we are able to think about the general ways in which algorithms are complicit in processes of social ordering and control. Cheney-Lippold (2011: 166), for instance, directly connects issues of ordering and control to the categorisations that are made by sorting algorithms. The power here is in defining and differentiating us through data, which, in turn, creates normalising behaviours and identities (Cheney-Lippold, 2011: 177). Indeed, there are a number of arguments being made about the new forms of power that emerge in software dense infrastructures and algorithmically defined information flows. As might be expected, the ways that these new forms of social power operate fits into the questions about agency and iteration that we have already discussed. For example, a common power associated with algorithms and software concerns the ability of companies and organisations to track and trace individuals and groups. The result is the often discussed ability of companies to harvest data and to make predictions about people. For instance, Crang and Graham (2007: 811–812) say that:

> Consumer technologies are also clearly designed to make our preferences for, uses of, and indeed thoughts about, products traceable. In the newly visible field of practices they, too, can then deploy algorithmic agency to target the most appropriate or profitable consumer.
>
> (Crang and Graham, 2007: 811–812)

Again we find the constitutive power of these systems outlined. Here these systems make preferences visible to organisations so that they can then act on these newly visible consumer patterns. The result is that capitalists can target consumers by using the predictive capacities of the new digital architectures of consumption. The form of social power operating here is about selection, about who gets targeted, who gets preferential treatment and who is looked upon favourably (Graham, 2004c). This might seem minor, and indeed the attention of being targeted might be unwelcome, but in some instance being targeted and viewed preferentially might actually play closely with life opportunities, comfort and even social mobility, if, for example, the products are financial services, healthcare services, or insurance (Burrows and Ellison, 2004).

Indeed, there seems a general consensus that 'code is altering the nature of consumption' (Kitchin and Dodge, 2011: 210). In fact there is a good deal of literature now emerging about new forms of consumer capitalism in an age of predictive algorithms and software-centred consumption practices (Thrift, 2005; Turow 2006). This change in the nature of consumer capitalism is illustrative of the almost unimaginable power of algorithms in the global economy. For example, Kitchin and Dodge (2011: 210) have observed that:

Software has led to the virtual abstraction of money, enabling finance to circulate through dense, interconnected and interdependent network of companies, products, and property, and creating new, fictitious, and speculative capital which is highly mobile. As a consequence, capta and software algorithms are at the heart of the global financial system, underpinning how monies were and continue to be, monitored, transferred, tracked, repackaged, sold, and leveraged

Kitchin and Dodge's position is that software, code and algorithms are at the centre of the functioning of consumer capitalism. Indeed, the economy couldn't actually function without them. This begins to give us a sense of the scale of the social ordering powers of algorithms, their reach into everyday processes and their embedded functioning in everyday life. Kitchin and Dodge take such observations far beyond this more abstract account of the flow of finance and the large-scale circuits of consumer capitalism to embed such ideas in the mundane environment of the home. They argue that: 'Every home is a node in multiple consumer and government networks relating to utilities, entertainment, communications, finance, taxation, health, and security, some of which work in real time, others asynchronously, all using electronic captabases structured and worked upon by software algorithms' (Kitchin and Dodge, 2011: 169).

In short, such large-scale functioning is networked into homespace (Dodge and Kitchin, 2009; see also McKelvey, 2010). These homes are also judged and defined by the algorithmic processes of which they are a part. This can relate to the way that the home is monitored for utilities and the like, but there is also a software density within the home that they have described, populated as they often are by various devices that require software and algorithms in order to function (see Chapter 2). What Kitchin and Dodge do here is to show the various scales of analysis that are required in understanding software and algorithmic processes, and how these different scales indicate the large-scale and small-scale power of algorithms in everyday life.

We might wonder though why this type of vast embeddedness of algorithms is actually also about new forms of social ordering and control. I've provided some outlines of this already in the chapter, and we will turn to culture in a moment for some specific examples.

If, for the moment, we stick with these broader themes, then Kitchin and Dodge provide us with some analytical pointers for unpicking algorithmic social ordering. They claim that there are 'grammars of action' within software code, and these have various outcomes that implicitly intervene in social ordering and control. Kitchin and Dodge (2011: 109) argue that the 'grammars of action of code increases the power of traditional ... surveillance and also actively reshapes behavior, creating automated capture systems in which software algorithms work automatically and autonomously'. Here we see multiple types of levels of social ordering occurring through software algorithms. They note that these algorithms help to increase visibility and thus expand the possibilities of traditional forms of surveillance. These algorithms are actively reshaping behaviour, as we have already seen in the above sections on agency and recursivity. And finally, importantly, algorithms work to capture and respond to social behaviours and actions in automated and unseen ways. This final issue means that algorithms, as has been shown elsewhere (Lash, 2007; Thrift, 2005; Hayles, 2006), order the world in ways that are often not even visible.

Again Louise Amoore's work is instructive in revealing exactly how these invisible processes work on the ground. Her suggestion is that algorithms work by focusing attention on specific things. The power of the algorithm is to draw attention to a desired focal point, thus obscuring the other possibilities. This is about the way that algorithms direct and guide encounters and decision-making. To be more exact, Amoore (2009a: 22) argues that:

> In effect, algorithms precisely function 'as a means of directing and disciplining attention, focusing on specific points and cancelling out all other data, appearing to make it possible to translate *probable* associations between people or objects into *actionable* security decisions

Selectivity and direction are the domain of algorithms. Algorithms highlight one point and in so doing mask others. And then on top of this, algorithmic systems make predictions and probable associations seem concrete, real and inevitable. This is to make a reality out of a set of predictions which then become the basis of decision-making. This might be decision-making about a myriad of things, including music choices and the like. Fans of cricket at this point, for example, might be thinking about the way that a simulation is used to predict the trajectory a cricket ball would have taken after hitting the batter's leg. Here a probable outcome is used to make a decision about whether the batter should be out leg-before-wicket or not (i.e. would the ball have carried on and hit the stumps). Here a prediction created by software algorithms becomes the basis of an actionable decision.

Indeed, for Amoore one of the key powers of algorithms is in the predictions of the future that they are used to make. These predictions, as we have suggested, become realities from which decisions are made. Thus the algorithm shapes decision-making processes with very real implications for individuals and how they are treated. Amoore (2009a: 22) explains that '[b]y connecting the dots of probabilistic associations, the algorithm becomes a means of foreseeing or anticipating a course of events yet to take place'. These 'lines of sight' are powerful in shaping all sorts of decisions. Again, in the security setting they are a way of predicting levels of risk and acting on such predictions. For Amoore, this signals an important change in decision-making processes and in the types of resources used to make judgements about people, with new types of data fusing with new algorithmic decision-making processes. As Amoore (2009b: 53) puts it:

> The deployment of algorithmic calculations in this context signals an important move – from the effort to predict future trends on the basis of fixed statistical data to a means of pre-empting the future, drawing probable futures into imminent and immediate commercial decision.

Amoore's point is that such processes need to be understood in order to understand the implications they have for decision-making. Clearly there is a widespread and significant presence of algorithms shaping such judgements. In turn these have material outcomes for those who are making and those who are on the receiving end of such decisions. This 'anticipatory knowledge' (Kinsley, 2012: 1562–1564) has come to be very powerful in the security sector. Kinsley (2012) argues that a critical response to the use of such knowledge is crucial (see also Knox and Harvey, 2011). The algorithms here are powerful in making predictions that then classify and order people, and then ultimately shape how they are treated and what type of response they receive. Undoubtedly then there is a politics of algorithms on display in Amoore's work. For Amoore (2009a: 22) these represent a 'mode of calculation' based upon the sharing of data between agencies, with the algorithm producing a 'visualization of suspicion' that then feeds into judgements about how other people are judged. The roots of these systems return us back to consumer capitalism, as the 'origins of algorithmic techniques for visualizing people lie, perhaps not surprisingly, in commercial techniques for imagining the consumer' (Amoore, 2009a: 22). We are seeing then the same types of algorithmically defined decision-making and prediction about individuals across various sectors.

We can only then, based on Amoore's work, begin to imagine how we, as consumers, are being analysed (for example see Beer, 2010). As well as thinking through the issues associated with the highlighting of certain possibilities and the power of prediction in shaping decisions, Amoore also describes how algorithms become powerful in making and shaping social norms and perceptions of appropriate or ordinary behaviours. Amoore argues that '[m]odes of attentiveness in contemporary homeland security practice ... are particularly dependent on algorithmic logics that designate anomaly on the basis of a screening of the norm' (Amoore, 2009a: 25). The algorithms use the data to make judgements against such social norms. Those who do not display such norms are highlighted as holding abnormal properties. We can imagine, when we think of how these systems are being used across sectors, how powerful these embedded norms might be. Jordan Crandall similarly claims (2010: 71) that algorithms are powerful, often through the analysis of risk in surveillance, in that they 'construct the norm'.

So on the surface algorithms might appear to be neutral decision-makers. It would seem though that this is far from being the case. Rather they are active in normalising behaviour patterns and in making predictions about the perceived adherence to norms based upon certain data sets. Finally, Amoore points out that '[w]hile they appear to visualize a picture of a person that is culturally nuanced – every minute and prosaic "behaviour", every aspect of a way of life potentially becoming a part of the classification – they actually efface difference in their drive for identification' (Amoore, 2009a: 24). So whilst we might think of algorithms, in the security and border services as well as in consumer culture, as providing tailored and individual responses, they are in fact often making judgements about groups and the norms of those groups. They are judging not that individual but making deductions based upon the data about other groups of individuals.

Some of the decisions that shape everyday lives need not be as obviously significant as those taken by border guards. Even, according to Kitchin and Dodge (2011), familiar and routine software 'applications like Microsoft Word or Adobe Photoshop are flexible and open-ended tools, but they come loaded up with structures, templates, default settings, algorithmic normalities and path dependencies that often subtly but necessarily direct users to certain solutions' (Kitchin and Dodge, 2011: 122). Perhaps we can add other familiar software applications such as PowerPoint, Google Scholar, Atlas.ti, NVivo, LexisNexis, SPAD and SPSS (on the latter see Uprichard et al., 2009). We can imagine that these all come with such algorithmic normalities that frame the outputs of academics and direct us to certain solutions. There is some scope here for thinking of the power of algorithms in academic research, with these underpinning software gently shaping what it is that academics produce, what they find out, what they see in their data and how they perform their work. The central point though is that even these fundamentally ordinary software applications are subtly framing everyday practices. The outcome is that we can begin to see the scale of algorithmic sorting not just in cultural consumption, but also in the making and finishing of cultural products.

I have already described briefly how Mager's work explores the algorithmic shaping of behaviour. But when considering how algorithms play a part in social ordering processes it is perhaps important to reiterate how 'capitalist ideology gets inscribed in search algorithms by way of social practices' (Mager, 2012: 770). This is to think of algorithms not as neutral mathematical forces that simply do a job but to return again to the earlier point about the social models that are used to design algorithms. It is to presume that dominant capitalist ideologies become a part of how algorithms themselves are designed and the functions they perform. This, for Mager, is about how capitalism 'gets aligned with and woven into the mathematics of search algorithms and how website providers and users comply with and stabilize this dynamic' (Mager, 2012: 770). Capitalist spirit, she argues, gets 'inscribed in the fabric of search algorithms by way of social practices' (Mager, 2012: 782). Galloway (2011: 100) indirectly draws a similar conclusion by noting that there 'is one game in town: a positivistic dominant of reductive, systemic efficiency and expediency'. The values of capitalism, famously described by Lyotard (1979) as the minimum input maximum output performativity equation, are inscribed on to the design and functioning of the algorithm. The pursuit of the increasingly perfect predictive algorithm in the Netflix competition with which I opened this chapter, serves as an illustrative example here. It is helpful to return to Adrian Mackenzie's (2006) work here to think of this ideology of capitalism as being a part of the models that frame and instruct algorithmic design. In this parallel work Mackenzie and Vurdubakis (2011: 4) also suggest that code and algorithms need to be understood 'not only in terms of software but also in terms of cultural, moral, ethical and legal codes of conduct'.

As this all indicates, there are also some very mundane and everyday ways in which algorithms perform an ordering function. Here the power of algorithms is in shaping what or who is visible. Again, the issue of the type of material we encounter is important. Taina Bucher (2012) has argued that social networking sites like Facebook are the site of algorithmic power where the threat of invisibility leads to certain types of activities and behaviours. It is of course the algorithmic processes that define visibility in these spaces. As with Amoore's work, the algorithms in social networking sites are intended to make behaviours visible, but in this instance the outcomes are more publicly visible and desired. People want to be visible and so they play to the 'algorithmic architectures'. Bucher's study shows how the 'news feed' on Facebook, which is a stream of information about the things your social network of 'friends' are up to, is an algorithmic sorting process that makes decisions about what and who should grab the headlines and thus be more visible. In this instance the EdgeRank algorithm uses various features to filter the news alerts. These include the level of interaction between the two friends, the type of interaction, how important that type of interaction is deemed to be and the 'time decay' or how fresh the news is (Bucher, 2012: 4). One of Bucher's claims is that the power of this algorithm to make things visible is at the same time a powerful force in promoting the threat of invisibility in these spaces, with visibility being a kind of reward for being active and interacting frequently. Bucher's work shows then how algorithms are central to the operation and behaviours we might find on Facebook, which, given its population, reveals just how deeply embedded algorithms are in everyday cultural practices and interactions.

Algorithms, cultural encounters and the shaping of taste

There has been a good deal of talk in the social sciences about the importance of cultural tastes and preferences. This literature outlines the part that tastes and preferences in culture play in fostering social connections and divisions, in making social class, in building and maintaining social hierarchies and networks, in catalysing group formation and friendships, in defining positions in fields, in affording or denying social mobility and the like (see for example Bennett et al., 2009). These types of debates have re-emerged recently with some strength through the rejuvenation of the analysis of the class/culture nexus and the renewed interest in the application of Pierre Bourdieu's analytical frameworks (Bennett et al., 2009). Despite this interest, virtually no attention has been given to how cultural infrastructures and emergent media forms might be shaping, guiding and reshaping these apparently important cultural tastes and preferences. As a result we might be missing an important dimension from such analyses of the social ordering powers of culture. Indeed, it might even be the case that some of the discussions about cultural omnivorousness (Savage and Gayo, 2011) and the like are missing out on one of the crucial dimensions that is now responsible for the formation of taste. This is not to say that social class and personal networks do not shape taste anymore, but that ultimately we may find in new media infrastructures powerful forces that implicate the direction of cultural tastes. For example, and to foreground the argument, it might be that tastes amongst a group are eclectic or, to use the post-bourdieusian language, omnivorous, because algorithms guide them towards such taste formations. As such, the following argument might ask questions about our understanding of the causality of culture. Reflecting on the previous discussions of algorithmic agency, recursivity and power, the chapter now attempts to open up this issue for further elaboration.

Of course, one of the most visible forms of algorithmic recommendation comes from the highly popular online retailer Amazon.

Amazon is now highly familiar and has been widely commented on. Amazon, as we know, recommends book, music and film purchases based on purchasing profiles. As Kitchin and Dodge (2011:205) describe:

> Amazon's 'personalized recommendations' works on...tracking the browsing history, keyword searches, and purchases of individual customers to build a multi-dimensional profile of taste in reading or music or other consumer items, to then make recommendations for other purchases based on what other people with similar profiles have bought.

Amazon does not just have these automated recommendations, it also guides by showing what other people who viewed the item also purchased, by showing what percentage of people who bought the viewed item then went on to purchase, the list goes on. These all use data to algorithmically guide choice.

Back in the early 2000s Robert Spector (2002) wrote a short account of the early development of Amazon. This now provides a useful historical document of the approach that made Amazon a distinctive presence at the time of its publication. The book is obviously now out of date in terms of the technical aspects of the site, but it remains revealing in terms of the ethos underpinning the individual tailoring of the site for visitors, the strategies of predicting tastes and the making visible of other people's purchasing – thus building a number of feedback loops into the consumer experience. In particular, Spector's history outlines the attempt to hone customer experience around personalisation. The aims were to make the site increasingly efficient, rapid and functional (Spector, 2002: 126–157). Spector reflects on the early stages of the recommendation system, saying that as 'the site became more sophisticated, the service has become more personalized...The personalization is part of Amazon's philosophy of "mass customization"' (Spector, 2002: 142). Again we see this use of aggregate level knowledge of consumer patterns being used to indicate a personalisation, or mass personalisation, of the consumer experience. These, as Nigel Thrift (2005) has described, are classic rhetorics of 'knowing capitalism'.

Spector continues by describing the various developments in the recommendation of products to users of Amazon, and how these were honed in the early stages. Despite these developments being at a nascent stage, they highlight the centrality of personalisation and notions of shared taste in the processes from the outset. Apart from anything else, this shows the length of time that recommendation systems and the visibility of purchasing patterns of other people have now been enmeshed in consumption practices. Indeed we find that this type of 'knowing' ethos is built into the structures and cultures of this type of organisation. This is revealed by Spector (2002: 142) in a quote from an interview with Jeff Bezos, the founder of Amazon: 'I want to transport online bookselling...back to the days of the small bookseller, who got to know you very well and would say things like, "I know you like John Irving, and guess what, here's this new author, I think he's a lot like John Irving" '. The suggestion in this interview with Bezos is that Amazon effectively aimed to replace this type of 'knowing' form of consumer interaction, with human agency and knowledge central to the connections required for the personal recommendation to be made in the small shop, with the agency of algorithms and the knowledge extracted from large-scale data about consumption. Here algorithmic agency replaces human judgement and databases replace the accumulated tacit knowledge of an individual at work for years in a bookshop. Although we might of course question the rather quaint image that Bezos conjures in order to do this, we can still see the early direction and rhetorical construction of algorithmic systems.

To bring this story up to date, as I was compiling this chapter Amazon launched a new service which it called Amazon Cloud Player. In line with other forms of cloud computing, the idea is that music collections are no longer stored on a single device, but rather they exist in 'the cloud' and can therefore be accessed from any web enabled device – a classic Web 2.0 approach towards storage (see Beer and Burrows, 2007). This service enables all music purchased on Amazon, as well as other imported music from iTunes and the like, to be securely stored on Amazon. The pitch that accompanies this development suggests that the user need no longer worry about storing their music, nor need they worry about their music collection being a 'bit messy'. The new facility is presented as a solution to such problems, as it allows a consolidation of music into one accessible space. We can imagine though that what we also get here is a space that has a very comprehensive ability to capture music listening practices. The result of which is that Amazon will in turn be honing the data resources that then feed back into their predictive analytics and recommendation system. It is at this point that the capabilities and functioning, presented through capitalist rhetoric, begin to mesh with design futurism to 'make' particular futures (Kinsley, 2012). This example illustrates how such 'circuits of capitalism' (Thrift, 2005) are central to the generation of value in these media forms. Again, expanding the ability to extract by-product data becomes a part of the development of the site.

The inclusion of personalised processes in consumer capitalism has received quite a bit of attention over recent years, but the ways in which this now familiar recommendation system might be intervening in the formation of taste and preferences has received much less attention. Returning to Amoore's work, the power of algorithms is in focusing the attention and in highlighting particular focal points. As with decision-making about risk factors, here recommendations present actionable decisions based on probable associations, as Amoore put it. The recommendation algorithms draw the attention towards particular cultural products and thus exercise the power to shape cultural encounters that then feed into taste. This has not really seeped over into work on cultural taste, although it is undoubtedly now a prominent part of consumer culture. As things stand the exact part that something like the Amazon recommendation system plays in taste formation is unclear.

Such cultural algorithmic processes reach far beyond these more visible recommendation systems. When searching on Google we see what other people with similar search terms searched for, we get pingbacks showing us who is talking about our blog entries, we can see what is trending on Twitter, we can even get academic articles recommended to us on Google Scholar. Each of these processes uses the feedback of data and algorithmic selection and visibility processes to order culture, drawing attention to certain things and away from others, and often providing real-time accounts of what is hot (see Chapter 5). It is now common to find that even broadcast media, such as TV shows, are commented upon via Twitter, with presenters sometimes even revealing in real-time how their show is being received by Twitter users. The list of such algorithmically refined feedbacks of data into culture are massive once we look across the different circulations of data that inform us of what is going on around us or that enable the culture to 'find us'.

The recommendation systems of prediction, as with Amazon and Netflix, are, despite being familiar and automated, in some ways the most visible aspects of 'knowing capitalism' (Thrift, 2005) in culture. To take another example, Genius is the predictive arm of Apple's ubiquitous iTunes software (Beer, 2010). Genius allows users to find music that they might like on iTunes, based not just upon their purchasing profile but also on the basis of the music they have actually listened to (which is captured by the devices and software). Here the predictions make connections based upon iTune's vast accumulated data about its millions of users worldwide. A similar application of this type of predictive algorithm can be found on the music site Last.fm. This site uses the data 'scrobbled' – which is the data harvested from devices – to build up a profile and make selections of music to listen to based upon the profile. As with Amoore's observations about such processes appearing to be individually tailored but actually being about the aggregate level analysis, such processes are described as being about helping us to find music that suits us. Genius and Last.fm both use algorithmic predictive processes to highlight music and to guide users towards particular songs. Thus these algorithms have a significant power in shaping cultural encounters, in making cultural connections and in highlighting some music and thus relegating other music. The influence that this has on the cultural landscape of individuals can only be significant when we imagine the scale of the use of such systems, and when we begin to add together some of the most prominent means of cultural consumption in iTunes, Amazon and the like. There are also now numerous 'apps' emerging that use algorithms to help the music to 'find us'. Some use purchasing or listening profiles, others find similarities in the structures or sounds of the songs themselves to make these connections.

In other words, these systems are now a routine part of consumer culture. In some ways their influence is now so deeply embedded and often unseen that it is increasingly hard to imagine or describe the impact that algorithms might be having on cultural encounters, tastes, preferences and subsequently on communities, groups, networks and movements. They are already almost too numerous to describe or list. If cultural encounters are shaped by culture finding-us, then we might imagine that this will complicate any kind of reductive vision of how cultural capital might be accumulated. If this cultural knowledge now finds-us, then cultural know-how might be decoupled from the types of socialisation processes that are more dependent on friendship groups and the consumption of the right type of broadcast media outputs. We might wonder where this might leave something like Sarah Thornton's (1995) notion of 'subcultural capital', if these forms of knowledge can now circulate outside of subcultural groups and as they find a new audience through algorithmic processes.

We now need some more comprehensive studies that make some attempt to understand how these algorithmic new media infrastructures are coming to shape tastes and preferences. These would need to explore how these systems intervene in some of the social connections and divisions that we have long understood to be linked into expressions of taste. I have mentioned two examples from music in iTunes and Last.fm. Amazon deals with a more wide ranging scope of consumer purchases from DVDs, to music, to film, games and games consoles and even clothing. Then we can add the types of networked hard-drive based smart television systems and watch on demand services provided by many channels. I also mentioned the Netflix example; other on demand web-based services are taking on a new presence even in mainstream and public broadcasting. Similarly in literature, iTunes and Amazon are influential, particularly with Amazon's Kindle e-readers, but also stretching into academia we can consider how other digital literature is finding its audience through news feeds on academia.edu and the developments that are occurring around Google Scholar and what look to be new 'apps' that mean that academic articles will now begin to find researchers based upon their reading and/or publishing profiles. As Kitchin and Dodge (2011: 205) argue, this 'kind of analysis is only feasible with the scalability and automation offered by coded, algorithmic processing'.

Of course, as a rejoinder, we might wonder if and how people respond to the recommendations they are presented with. Do they take them up? Do they see them as being relevant and helpful? Do they respond critically? This is the point when human agency rubs up against algorithmic agency. The important point though is that it is the algorithmic agency that is deciding what it is that the individual encounters, and what it is that they are making a decision about. Their interaction with that capitalist organisation is algorithmically defined and so is the cultural opportunity it affords. This is where we might return to the points raised earlier about the power of algorithms in making certain objects more visible, as with Bucher's work on Facebook and Amoore's and Crandall's on tracking and risk assessment. Here it is about the visibility of culture, and of particular forms of culture that algorithmically finds its audience. These systems shape cultural encounters and cultural landscapes. They also often act to make taste visible. The question this creates is about the power of algorithms in culture and, more specifically, the power of algorithms in the formation of tastes and preferences. When we look, as we increasingly do in the analysis of culture, to work exploring taste, we often see taste expressed in acts of consumption. But these expressions in acts of consumption might not be originating from the same pathways and resources that we might imagine. At least the origins of taste formation may now be, at least in part, algorithmically shaped by these new media infrastructures as they come to dominate popular culture. To take an example, behind every multiple correspondence analysis diagram depicting taste clusterings (see for example Le Roux et al., 2008) there could be algorithmic processes lurking in the shadows, shaping those clusters by influencing cultural knowledge, tastes and preferences. Perhaps this is not just about cultural know-how and social capital, perhaps it is something much more material that is now a structural part of how culture is encountered, consumed and disseminated. There are a new set of agencies mixing in these processes that are actively having a say in the formation of cultural know-how. Algorithms are also drawing cultural boundaries and influencing where these boundaries are placed and where divisions occur. The observation we are led towards, by looking across at work in bioinformatics, border control and computer science, is that in the case of culture, as it follows the types of processes prevalent in other spheres, we need now to pay attention to what might be thought of as *the infrastructures of taste formation* and to a potential shift in the ontology of taste formation.

Conclusion: opening up the missing dimensions and dynamics of cultural taste

Given the above discussions it is perhaps not surprising that software algorithms have been described as 'a vital source of social power' (Kitchin and Dodge, 2011: 246). The obvious outcome of this observation is a call for us to 'to prise open the black boxes of algorithms...to understand software as a new media that augments and automates society' (Kitchin and Dodge, 2011: 246). This is required, so the argument goes, in order for us to understand this concealed social power in operation. As Steve Graham has recognised, 'the algorithms that support...choices, simulations, orderings, and classifications...remain completely and utterly unscrutinized' (Graham, 2005: 10). Things have shifted in the last seven or eight years, and as a result Graham's claim that they are 'utterly unscrutinized' no longer entirely pertains, indeed I have shown a range of work here in which algorithms and software are at the forefront of the analysis. There still remains though a need for us to get to the 'very guts' (Graham, 2005: 10) of these systems. In culture, for instance, there is very little work on the social and sorting power of algorithms. This needs to be addressed, and opening this project up has been the main objective of this chapter.

Developing their broader project, Kitchin and Dodge have argued that '[t]here is also a need to develop a sub-area of software studies – algorithm studies – that carefully unpicks the ways in which algorithms are products of knowledge about the world and how they produce knowledge that then is applied, altering the world in a recursive fashion' (Kitchin and Dodge, 2011: 248). This chapter has hoped to demonstrate that this vision for algorithmic studies is needed in the study of culture and particularly popular culture. This is no easy task, because, as Graham points out, 'the worlds of software-sorting tend not to be amenable in any meaningful way to traditional geographical or social scientific research techniques or conceptualizations' (Graham, 2005: 15). The same applies to the study of culture; we have few methodological or conceptual points of reference for such a development of the study of algorithms in culture. I hope that the exploration of conceptual ideas around algorithms in this chapter, as applied to culture, offers a vocabulary and framework for developing such a set of analytical approaches.

As part of this set of developments, and to locate a way to continue with such a project, we can turn again to Kitchin and Dodge's (2011: 255) important book. They conclude that what is needed is a 'genealogy of algorithms'. As they add:

> We believe it would be instructive to conduct a detailed archeology of how algorithms come to be constructed – to excavate the social

lives of ideas into code – and how an algorithm then translates
and mutates across projects to be reemployed in diverse ways.
(Kitchin and Dodge, 2011: 255)

It is such a vision of an archaeology or genealogy of algorithms
that needs to be developed in cultural analysis in order for a more
complete vision of contemporary culture and contemporary popular
culture to be developed. This is not something that can simply be
developed in one book chapter, rather this is an ongoing task that
will need resources and time. If algorithmic systems are ignored we
may come to know very little about the actual functioning of culture
in the everyday setting, particularly as software and algorithms come
to define more and more aspects of how culture is made, disseminated and consumed. Popular culture, to use Kitchin and Dodge's
(2011) terminology, is 'code/space', it relies on software and algorithms to function, and therefore this functioning needs to be part of
the analysis. The issues of agency, visibility and prediction have been
discussed here as key problems within this project.

Perhaps the most important observation to take away into an
understanding of culture is that algorithms do not just predict. Algorithms have the capacity and potential to *make taste* by shaping
cultural encounters and crafting our cultural landscapes. They are,
as Morris (2012) put it, prescriptive as well as descriptive. As such
there is some suggestion that the very ontology of taste formation may be altering. These recommendations and encounters will
inevitably become self-fulfilling prophecies as they continue to shape
our cultural landscapes and the things we come across. This then, as
Sterne (2012) notes in his detailed account of the culturally defining MP3 format, is an 'algorithmic culture'. If this is the case then
it is crucial that we begin to see how algorithms implicate culture.
This potentially requires us to revisit some of our understandings
of the ways that culture is organised and how it feeds into social
relations. In this chapter, using a range of literature from various
disciplines, I hope I have shown that there are various social dimensions to algorithms that are now likely, given the prominence of
new media infrastructures in cultural production and consumption,
to be altering aspects of cultural engagement and circulation. There
is something of a changing ontology of taste formation being intimated here. Not least we are forced to wonder what this means for our

understandings of the role of cultural tastes and preferences in social divisions and social ordering. What, for example, do predictive algorithms mean for a concept like cultural capital if we are now able to experience cultural encounters algorithmically rather than as a pre-formed path of socialisation? Also, we might wonder what predictive algorithms might mean for social network analysis if they intervene in the foci that facilitate social connections? The list continues, what this chapter has sought to do is to raise such questions for further consideration, and in so doing lay out a set of conceptual touchstones for developing just such an agenda in the study of culture. However these technologies develop, algorithms are already deeply implicated in the manipulation of the circulations of data within and through popular culture.

5
Data Play: Circulating for Fun

Introduction: The value of data

Of all the developments at the crossover between new media and popular culture, it is probably Facebook that has received the most attention. This is understandable given the size of its population of users, the Hollywood film about its origins (*The Social Network*, 2010) and the massive media coverage it has received. As I write this chapter, the current news stories are about Facebook becoming a public company and its shares being opened up to trading. This share sale shows how data, in the form of the individual profiles of each of its users, are translated into monetary value. There have been lots of estimates of Facebook's value over the years, but this has now turned into an actual share price. According to reports, the first day's trading effectively valued the company at $104bn or £66bn (Rushe, 2012). What is important here is to note that the value of Facebook is in its data. It, of course, has other assets, but its high valuation comes from these 900 million or so individual profiles. As indication of this, Facebook's share price has been compared to other companies; as one report puts it:

> As with Google, there has been much scepticism about Facebook's ability to turn its phenomenal number of users into a business able to support a $100bn-plus valuation. Facebook's revenues were £3.7bn last year. Goldman Sachs, the investment bank, had revenues of nearly $29bn and its value is half of that of Facebook.
>
> (Rushe, 2012: 30)

The suggestion here is that the value of Facebook is not in the annual revenues it generates, but it is in the perceived value of its data. That is to say that the valuation of the company is a measure of the value of the data held in its archive of personal profiles. These, after all, are a dream for those interested in targeted advertising, predictive analytics and the like. The value of Facebook, however volatile this is turning out to be, is a product of those who have built the profiles and established networks. In other words, the infrastructure of participation (see Chapter 3) is provided by Facebook, the data generated and held within this archive are the product of the individual user – or 'prosumer' (see Ritzer and Jurgenson, 2012; see also Chapter 3).

This is where this chapter on data play begins, with the notion that these mediascapes are based upon participation. This participation might also be understood as a form of labour and value creation. The chapter begins by turning to a growing set of literature that talks about new media in these terms, with this creation of data being conceptualised as a form of 'free labour' (Terranova, 2000). From this point the chapter then moves towards thinking of this as a form of playful labour, with people not just generating data but also playing with it. The chapter develops the concept of *data play* to explore such practices. To make this vision more specific the chapter outlines some different types of data play before focusing upon a specific set of developments that might be thought of as an emergent culture of visualisation. It then concludes with some thoughts on what these observations mean for the study of culture. The central argument of this chapter is that data circulates back into culture through various forms of play, these are now integral parts of contemporary popular culture.

The social factory in popular culture

A good deal of recent writings on work and labour have spoken of the stretching of work across the time and space of everyday life (Gill and Pratt, 2008; Gregg, 2011). This stretching has been associated with a general shift towards forms of precarious, temporary or immaterial labour afforded by new working cultures and developments in communications technologies. Much of this work is concerned with how work stretches into leisure time, thus blurring the boundaries between the two. We can take Ros Gill and Andy Pratt's (2008) work as a general starting point. Their argument, focusing upon workers in the creative and cultural industries, is that there are new forms of 'precarious labour' emerging that may in turn lead to new forms of solidarity. Gill and Pratt's claim, is that in order to understand such labour we need to focus upon the subjectivity of these workers to see the meanings they attach to the work and the affects that these working patterns and demands have emotionally, physically and socially. At the core of their argument is the notion of the 'social factory', in which the walls around work break down as sporadic working patterns, the need to network and socialise, the competition for the next contract, anxiety and the technological networking of workers lead to the expansion of work across everyday life. Gill and Pratt (2008) turn to Tronti's much earlier concept of the 'social factory'. From this perspective, they say, 'labour is deterritorialized, dispersed and decentralized' (Gill and Pratt, 2008: 7). The social factory then is a concept concerned with understanding how the walls of the factory expand outwards (Negri in Gill and Pratt, 2008: 7).

As this suggests, the social factory argument is about the nature of work time and how it blends with off time. The reverse case has also been argued, and is gaining increasing weight and credibility, which is that fun and entertainment, and popular culture more generally, are increasingly based around forms of 'free' or 'digital' labour (Scholz, 2012). Indeed, it is not too much of a stretch to see how the type of blurring between production and consumption discussed in Chapter 3, and often understood through the notion of the prosumer, might be seen as being a form of work (Ritzer and Jurgenson, 2010). And, of course, we now also have the monetary values attached to Facebook's shares to suggest the value that such productive labour is generating.

Much of this work has been influenced by Tiziana Terranova's (2000) prophetic article 'Free Labor: producing culture for the digital economy'. Clearly there have been some significant changes in digital culture in the last 12 years, but despite these apparent changes much has been made of Terranova's account of the part that 'free labor' plays in what was then an emerging digital economy. In this influential article Terranova (2000: 33) argued that:

The NetSlaves are not simply a typical form of labor on the Internet; they also embody a complex relation to labor that is widespread in late capitalist societies... I understand this relationship as a provision of 'free labor,' a trait of the cultural economy at large, and an important, and yet undervalued, force in advanced capitalist societies. By looking at the internet as a specific instance of the fundamental role played by free labor, this essay also tries to highlight the connections between the 'digital economy' and what Italian autonomists have called the 'social factory'.

The basic premise here then is that parts of the contemporary economy are built upon this free labour. The example of Facebook with which I opened this chapter is particularly illustrative of this production of value through free forms of labour. Terranova's descriptions of the types of free labour that were occurring are understandably a little dated, but in many ways the basic premise has become more prominent with the rise of decentralised media networks, the open source movement (mentioned by Terranova but which has escalated since) and the even more powerful rise of social media platforms (Scholz, 2012; again see Chapter 3 for the inclusion of the organisation of content in this labour). Terranova (2000: 33–34) explains that:

> Simultaneously voluntarily given and unwaged, enjoyed and exploited, free labor on the Net includes the activity of building Web sites, modifying software packages, reading and participating in mailing lists, and building virtual spaces on MUDs and MOOs. Far from being an 'unreal,' empty space, the Internet is animated by cultural and technical labor through and through, a continuous production of value that is completely immanent to the flows of the network society at large.

It is important not to get distracted here by Terranova's talks of older formats such as MUDS and mailing lists, clearly the central idea resonates with developments in user generated content and the like. Before moving on to look at this let us just dwell for a moment on the detail of Terranova's position. It is important to note that Terranova is pointing towards a wide range of activities in her discussion of free labour – seemingly because these quite banal activities that we wouldn't necessarily think of as labour are responsible for generating value for capitalist organisations. As the following passage indicates:

This essay describes the digital economy as a specific mechanism of internal 'capture' of larger pools of social and cultural knowledge. The digital economy is an important area of experimentation with value and free cultural/affective labor. It is about specific forms of production (Web design, multimedia production, digital services and so on), but is also about forms of labor we do not immediately recognize as such: chat, real-life stories, mailing lists, amateur news letters and so on.

(Terranova, 2000: 38)

Terranova appears keen to explicate this sense of labouring in the digital economy in order to help us to understand the relations between routine web-based cultural and communicative activities and the development of capitalism. Some of these activities are more obviously forms of labour, but all are contributing to creating value. We can immediately see here why there is such potential in Terranova's observations; indeed the above passage would be far easier to write today with so much of the web content being created by users. This fits into this second category of things that are labour but which are not necessarily seen as such. Terranova (2000: 48) could not have seen how accurate her point that the 'sustainability of the Internet as a medium depends on massive amounts of labor' would become.

It is perhaps not surprising that Terranova's (2000: 38–39) argument is that 'cultural flows' originate 'within a field', and that capitalism is not just about incorporation but is 'immanent', it is occurring within these cultures (in some ways then foreshadowing the arguments about immanence made by Scott Lash, 2002). Terranova's central observations are then used to explore a range of issues concerning conceptions of production and consumption, of material and immaterial labour and the like. For example, she instructively argues that, against any obvious and crude reading of the situation, 'free labor ... is not necessarily exploited labor' (Terranova, 2000: 48). It is interesting that the argument here guides us away from a simple tendency to equate labour with exploitation, a point that has been followed up on by Hesmondhalgh (2010: 273–276). Rather Terranova explores the way that value is extracted from the seduction of participation in these environments. The extraction of value spreads to the work of those who perhaps are not usually so productive for capitalist organisations, which she says:

> manage the impossible, creating monetary value out of the most reluctant members of the postmodern cultural economy: those who do not produce marketable style, who are not qualified enough to enter the fast paced world of the knowledge economy, are converted into monetary value through their capacity to perform their misery.
>
> (Terranova, 2000: 52)

The basic point is important, this web-based form of free labour extracts value from the activities of a wide range of individuals who are engaging in all sorts of practices. The problems here are with the depiction of these as being reluctant; it has instead been more recently argued that this is part of the seduction of consumer culture with which they are highly engaged (see Bauman, 2007).

We can sympathetically acknowledge that the descriptive aspects of Terranova's piece are a little dated, yet it still prophetically foresees the type of free labour that has drastically escalated in recent years. Indeed, there is an increasing body of work concerned with the types of questions about free labour and the digital economy that were posed by Terranova. These questions have only escalated in relevance in recent years and as the work of participation has become such a significant part of culture.

If we pick up on one stream of this work, we find that the presence of what is often referred to as user-generated content becomes the focus for the analysis of such labour. Hesmondhalgh (2010: 268) agrees with Terranova in suggesting that:

> It is certainly the case that the cultural industries in the digital era, like many other kinds of firm, increasingly seek to draw upon participation of their users and consumers. But too many of these discussions of transformations associated with new digital media rely on caricatured portrayals of supposedly bypassed eras...Clichés and received thinking seem to dominate this area of debate.

Of course, Hesmondhalgh's observation is important in terms of how we generate understandings of such media (for support of this see for example Manovich, 2001; Gane and Beer, 2008). The rise in social media is not a usurping of broadcast media (Poster, 1995), rather these things become entwined or remediated (Graham, 2004b). In celebrity gossip for instance, we see blogs and Twitter interweaving with magazines, TV and print news media. So we need to proceed with some caution with narratives about the sudden involvement of 'ordinary' people in media content generation (Turner, 2010).

The issue that Hesmondhalgh draws upon from Terranova concerns the understanding of exploitation in these relations. He attempts to expand upon the careful account of the issue of exploitation taken from Terranova, to argue that user-generated content need not be thought of simply in terms of worn debates in which labour is automatically linked to exploitation. Hesmondhalgh, of course, has a more solid base for making such claims, given that he is writing about something that is happening rather than, as in Terranova's case, something that will happen. Hesmondhalgh (2010: 276) concludes that the 'concept of "free labour" is linked to some interesting ideas about power and control in cultural production in the digital era. But the frequent pairing of the term with the concept of exploitation is unconvincing and rather incoherent'. For Hesmondhalgh there is much to be gained from such free labour. Add to this the changing nature of work more generally, and this means that a new type of conceptual approach is needed. This, of course, returns us to Gill and Pratt's accounts of solidarity in the social factory and Terranova's attempts to uncover the routines inherent to the digital economy. What's more, as we reflect on the descriptions of the creation of archives from Chapter 3 alongside the type of data play I discuss later in the chapter, we can see that recourse to simple understandings of these forms of free labour as exploitative does not fit all that well. This labour might be exploitative, but it is also a form of play and entertainment.

It is perhaps unsurprising, given the nature of contemporary media, that the issue of the co-creation of content as a form of collective labour is receiving increasing attention (see Scholz, 2012). For example, John Banks and Mark Deuze (2009), in a piece that introduces a special issue of the *International Journal of Cultural Studies* on the topic, provide an overview of work on free labour through the co-creation of media content. They suggest that part of the problem is that, as Hesmondhalgh also observes, much of the engagement has come from those who are essentially fans of these web cultures. This they juxtapose against much more detached and sterile accounts of media-based labour from academia. This, they allude, means that we have few satisfactory accounts of 'co-creative labour', as they call it. Banks and Deuze (2009: 422) argue for a more detailed analysis of the 'participants themselves', in the 'user-created content' and its 'circulation'. This, they point out, might help to avoid us being dragged into 'classical development *versus* dependency theories'. This is essentially an argument that we need to avoid simple distinctions about where the power lies in such environments, whether it be with the consumer or the capitalist organisation.

In an earlier piece, John Banks, this time writing with Sal Humphreys, shifts the focus to the relations between professionals and these amateur content creators (Banks and Humphreys, 2008). But again the underpinning argument is that we need to begin to see how capitalism and power structures are altered by this co-creation of content. This co-creative labour, they argue, is not simply exploitative but it 'wields its own form of power' that 'renegotiates' the relations of professionalism, knowledge, expertise and the like. Their argument is that these relations need to be scrutinised more closely to reveal the forms and impact of user-created content. Again, this communicates a necessity to explore a broader range of consequences of free labour. Following along similar lines, if in a slightly more conceptual direction, it has even been argued (Christian Fuchs, 2010), that this type of free labour, in the form of user-generated content, requires us to 'rethink the notion of class'.

Together what these various positions reveal, following from Terranova's important intervention, is that treating user-generated media content as a form of 'free labour' places this practice at the centre of some big questions about the nature of contemporary capitalism, production, consumption, exploitation, power and even social class. However we might feel about the credibility of such arguments, it is clear that this type of user-generated media content is a significant part of the generation of value in contemporary capitalism. However, as Hesmondhalgh (2010) makes clear, this needs to be considered with some caution given that much of contemporary capitalism works through more established and historically orientated means. Overall though there is a good deal of consensus emerging concerning the need to think of the creation of media content, which is now so prevalent in social media and social networking sites (see boyd and Ellison, 2007), as a form of free labour and as a part of the stretching of the walls of the social factory. It seems that social scientists are commonly finding that this challenges some of the conventional binaries between production and consumption or work and leisure. Thinking of such media participation as work paints it in a particular light, it pushes us towards questions of exploitation and the blurring of prior boundaries between a range of dualisms. This leaves us though with further work to do in order to understand the nature of this free labour and why it is that people are choosing, in large numbers, to participate in it. A simple observation at this juncture is that this type of labour is actually understood to be fun (Thrift, 2005: 1), it might even be felt to be an obligation of citizenship (Bauman, 2007). These are questions that might need to be explored elsewhere; let us focus instead on this occasion upon the types of work that are going on in the creation and circulation of popular culture, or what I call here *data play*.

Data play in the social factory

The above outline shows that data production in popular culture has been gaining increasing attention. As a result, it is being conceptualised in various ways, but these positions generally point towards culture as being the site of the production of valuable data. Thus data production through cultural engagement, central as it is to the digital economy, is seen as being part of the social factory; it is seen as a kind of work. This would be backed up by the valuations of Facebook and the size of archives like YouTube, Flickr and Instagram. Chapter 3 also indirectly showed how the production of organising metadata is also a form of labour that occurs within such archives of content. What has received less attention are the ways in which these data are played with, how they fold back to inform or entertain and how they are used to provide entertainment through their manipulation. Data play is also a form of activity or play that is occurring within the social factory. This has received less attention, yet this data play, as I call it, is a growing part of popular culture and of the digital economy. As such, the processes of free labour in the digital economy are far more diverse now than they might first have appeared to be. It is not just about creating content, it is also about how this content and its by-products fold back into culture.

One of the most visible forms of data folding back into popular culture occurs where web users observe or play with data, what I call here data play. This chapter treats this data play as a continuum activity that ranges from relatively passive forms, such as an interest in seeing 'what is hot' via real time charts and online aggregators, to more extreme and active forms of engagement where individuals are using various data sources to create sophisticated visualisations of culture. At one end of the spectrum then data play might be fairly routine or even passive. It might be embodied in an individual who wishes to find out what is going on in music culture, so they turn to the real-time charts on iTunes or Spotify to see what people are listening to and what is most popular at that moment. Here this form of data play is simply an attempt to look at the data and react to the charts. It might also be an individual using a data aggregator, something like HypeMachine, that tracks what people are saying about these artists, what the 'buzz' is around the music. It might be the individual using Google trends to see what people are searching for, the trending lists on Twitter, the most popular videos on YouTube or the annual reports of Google, Twitter and Facebook to see what is popular in the many charts and tables that are produced. These are types of data play, but they are quite passive, they don't require much engagement from the individual other than to access the charts, to make searches and to look at the different orders, tables or simple visuals. This is a playful engagement with data in circumstances where the basic analytics are already being performed and which can easily be accessed and used to inform cultural consumption. If we are thinking of this in terms of the social factory, then this is a part of the factory that requires little work.

The continuum can then shift towards more active forms of data play in which the individual becomes more involved in creating and analysing content. This can still be quite routine, and can still be something of a mainstream activity given the types of custom-built applications and interfaces that are available and the simplicity of the software. Here the individual may be creating a friend wheel on Facebook, or any of the other similar applications, to create a visualisation of their friendship networks. These visuals might then be shared and circulated through social media networks. Here these individuals are playing with the data generated by the individual friendship connections that are occurring in these spaces. The continuum of data play expands still further, with similar types of activities to this kind occurring in the data 'playgrounds' that accompany a number of social media sites. The music site Last.fm, for example, has its own data playground where it is possible to visualise taste communities, to compare your tastes with your friends, to create simple visuals comparing music tastes based on gender and age, or even to see how eclectic your music taste is compared to the population of users. These sites are often accompanied by data groups, blogs and forums where information is shared on how to play with the data and showcasing what is being produced – a kind of cannibalistic set of developments in which the sites both generate and encourage the re-use of the by-product data by its users.

This leads us to the more extreme end of the data play spectrum, in which more advanced forms of analysis are occurring amongst those with an interest in seeing what can be gained from the data, whether the interests are aesthetic, journalistic or simply for entertainment. At this extreme end, the various invitations to analyse the by-product data of popular culture are explored in some detail by those engaging in these web cultures. Here APIs are the currency, as Nathan Yau (2011: xv) observes:

> The collective web has also grown to be more open with thousands of Application Programming Interfaces (API) to encourage and entice developers to do something with all the available data. Applications such as Twitter and Flickr provide comprehensive APIs that enable completely different user interfaces from the actual sites. API cataloging site ProgrammableWeb reports more than 2,000 APIs.

The API has become the symbol of the appropriation of by-product data back into culture. The API is the form in which massive data sets are made available to be used in more advanced types of data play. These APIs are the resources used for this type of 'free labour' and the data play it represents. These are the raw data that then become the resources of data play of various types. The API, along with data playgrounds and the like, serve as a kind of invitation to work or 'playbour' (Kane, 2004) with the by-product data, to create

new materials. These new visuals often then circulate through practices of sharing, re-tweeting, re-blogging and the like. It is not just
notable that such data play makes use of these APIs, it is also interesting to note that these APIs are made available for this community
of players. This is an instantiation of the ideals or 'rhetoric of democ-
ratization' that has ushered in social media (Beer and Burrows, 2007;
Beer, 2009b) – for further examples of invitations to play with data
see data.gov.uk and data.gov. It should also be noted, of course, that,
on occasion, the more advanced forms of data play intersect with the
new passive forms, with 'interesting' visuals created by advanced data
play circulating through Tweets Blog posts and the like.

But what of the various forms of data play that we might place
across this continuum? In trying to capture a general sense of what
is happening here, the chapter focuses upon the more visual aspects
of these forms of data play to suggest that we can understand these
as being a part of a more general emergence of a culture of visualisation. This is a cultural shift that is interwoven with the emerging
affordances of media and the availability of data about culture.

The culture of visualisation

We can start by noting that data play is not an activity that is limited to what Turner (2010) describes as 'ordinary' people, it is also
something that is coming to define contemporary journalism. This is
driven not just by an interest in new forms of data, but also by an
interest in how the insights gained from such data might be communicated through visualisations of various types. To give an indicative
example, an interesting artefact is the recently developed open access
and open source *The Data Journalism Handbook* (Gray et al., 2012).
This book is a guide for journalists to find ways of telling stories out of
the new forms of digital data that are available. It notes the changing
nature of journalism, as journalists are faced with new opportunities
to use data, thus requiring new sets of skills and knowledge. The focus
is upon using 'infographics' to tell stories. Visualisation is described
in the guide as the 'workhorse' of data journalism. Visualisations are
seen as providing opportunities for telling of complex or technical
stories in a direct way, for finding stories in the data, for developing
new visual dimensions when reporting stories and so on.

In the social sciences, as in data journalism, it has been argued that
visualisations could play a central part in fostering a vibrant future

(Savage, 2009b). The suggestion though is not that social scientists should necessarily attempt to create these visuals for themselves, but rather that what is required is a creative and critical engagement with the visuals and visualisation techniques that already exist. As Savage (2009b: 171) has put it:

> The task of sociology might not be that of generating excep-tionally whizzy visuals, using the most powerful computers or an unprecedented comprehensive database, so much as subject-ing those which are routinely reproduced to critique and analysis. This involves making the deployment of these devices a subject of social science inquiry.

We can expand upon this conclusion by suggesting that there is a culture of visualisation emerging in popular culture, that is already significantly engaged in such a 'diagramatization of society' (Sav-age, 2009b: 171). In short, there are innumerable sociological, cul-tural and political visualisations being created and circulated that require the critical attention of social scientists (Crampton, 2009). This chapter notes the presence of a *culture of visualisation* that has emerged through a combination of the new possibilities of media and the emergence of new forms of digital data. It suggests that it is important that the social sciences attempt to critically engage with these cultures of visualisation in order to respond to their envision-ing of the social world. These are powerful visuals that are shaping perceptions of space, culture and social forces, we need to commen-tate on these developments, challenge these visions where necessary and perhaps even adapt and appropriate some of the more helpful techniques and visuals that are being produced.

The culture of visualisation I describe here appears to be inspired by a variety of motives, particularly as we look at the types of visuals that are being created. Some look to be virtuosic demonstrations of technical skill and knowledge, others look to be concerned with the aesthetic or artistic value of the imagery they create, while others seem to be engaging in a form of 'vernacular sociology' as they create descriptive analytics of social phenomena (Beer and Burrows, 2007, 2010b). These motivations are likely to be varied, but they contribute towards an increasing visibility of a visualised culture. So, on one side we have this *culture of visualisation* occurring, with people play-ing with data and visualisation techniques, on the other side what this is leading to is a large-scale *visualisation of culture*. This culture of visualisation can be thought of as an emergent interest in creating, engaging with and disseminating (sharing) visualisations of various types. There is a creativity and vibrancy in this play that not only informs visual techniques but which also identifies data sources that can be used to create these visuals. This culture of visualisation is encapsulated by this introduction to a public competition aimed at finding the best visualisation:

> Do you geek out on public data sets? Do you download the latest campaign donations data to see where candidates really stand? Do you eagerly await the latest census and public health data sets? Then this contest is for you! In cooperation with O'Reilly's Strata New York, the Tableau Software Interactive 'Viz' Contest will focus on government and public data... Find some data then use Tableau Public to analyze and visualize it. Submit your viz here... that's all it takes!.

This quote conjures the image of the more active members of the visualisation of culture, those playing with data, the 'geeks' who download and use data sets. A similar expression can be found through another data visualisation competition, the 'information is beautiful' awards http://www.informationisbeautifulawards.com/. This image of the dataviz geek is perhaps at the extreme end of what I am pointing towards here, the more active and immersed visualisation creator, but it is nonetheless indicative of a much wider cultural trend. In fact, to give an example, some readers, especially those who are admissions tutors, may have come across software for visualising data about university department recruitment patterns – apart from helping university admissions tutors, the software company Tableau Public is currently carrying visualisations of waste in the California court system, the commodities boom in Argentina and the pre-season predictions for American college football. Indeed, many of the recent developments in web cultures facilitate the production of some form of visualisation, and these visualisations then, if they catch attention, circulate through popular culture as they pass through social networks and patterns of sharing.

To find some further visible examples of this culture of visualisation, we need look no further than prominent and widely discussed official sites like data.gov or data.gov.uk to see that people are being actively encouraged to use social data to create visual insights. In these examples the motif of transparency in political rhetoric has been engendered in the public availability of previously protected data about populations (Ruppert, 2011). Elsewhere we have seen the impact in the UK of people playing with data about political expenses to reveal the activities of political figures. Ruppert and Savage (2012) have shown the way in which the culture of visualisation led to insights into these vast data on the expenses of UK politicians. Similarly, sociologists have also spoken of the rise of 'mashup' culture within which people are actively engaged in mashing together data sets to create visual insights of various types (Hardey and Burrows, 2008). Often these mashups take a data set and 'mash it' with Google maps to create some form of geographical representation (Crampton, 2009). Elsewhere visualisations like tag clouds have become quite a common sight, particularly for visualising the content of speeches and long articles (these are easy to create by simply importing text into applications like wordle.com to create a visual of the most commonly used words).

Many web applications are now set up for individuals to play with data, and there are often freely available applications to enable this. Again we return to the increasingly ubiquitous API. In a recently published guide to these popular visualisations, the statistician Nathan Yau pointed out that:

> With all this data sitting around in stores, warehouses, and databases, the field is ripe for people to make sense of it. The data itself isn't all that interesting (to most people). It's the information that comes out of the data. People want to know what their data says.

> (Yau, 2011: xv–xvi)

Yau's vision fits with the wider rhetoric of democratisation and participation that has ushered in many of these transformations in culture (for a critical account see Beer, 2009b). There are a variety of agents involved in seeing 'what their data says', some are created by 'ordinary' users playing with their own and others data, others by interns in organisations and others by professional visualisation creators. In fact there is something of a visualisation industry emerging. For an example of a professional 'information visualiser' the reader might be interested in Moritz Stefaner's work, for details of his projects and background see http://moritz.stefaner .eu/. These individuals are often trained statisticians and/or design-ers who appear to be working in the new economy created by the presence of new forms of data and the desire to see what these data say. The outputs of these professional visualisers are highly sophisticated and engaging. A visit to Moritz's site reveals an advanced set of practices that creatively elaborate data through mobile visuals. Academics might be interested in the various visuali-sations of academic citation counts and eigenfactors for example (see http://moritz.stefaner.eu/projects/eigenfactor/). There are a number of freelance data visualisers working in this emergent industry; other examples include Jan Willem Tulp (http://www.janwillemtulp.com/) and David McCandless (http://www.davidmccandless.com/) – their personal sites contain numerous examples of their visual works.

There are also sites like Many Eyes www-958.ibm.com/ designed to make visualisation practices available to wider web users, these carry applications that allow visitors to create their own visuali-sations or make available data sets for others to play with – this site offers an easy '3 step plan' for creating visualisations. This is in addition to the broader visual imaginary that is being deployed by those with the knowledge to do so. So we have some visualisa-tions facilitated by custom-built applications, and others who are actively using technical skills to create them. As a consequence, the aesthetic qualities of the visualisations vary somewhat, but on occasion there are some creative ideas to be found in even quite rudimentary visualisations. There are also sites dedicated to report-ing on such visualisations, of which flowingdata.com is probably the most comprehensive. This site acts as a portal or archive that gath-ers together images and links to the many visualising practices that are occurring. Some of these are visuals from official sources or from journalists wishing to create insights, others are more experimental, and some are simply comedic visual gags. To give an example, geo-commons.com produced a time specific map that shows the location of comments on Twitter concerning the royal wedding (the Duke and Duchess of Cambridge) during the 24 hour cycle on the 29th of April 2011 (see http://geocommons.com/maps/74215). It is possi-ble to watch this map play out over the day so that the location of the tweets can be seen through time. As this would suggest, such visualisations can be quite frivolous but they can also be used to deal with far-reaching social issues. The case of the recent social unrest in London (in the summer of 2011) is an interesting case here. In this instance data from various broadcast and social media sources were used to map the rioting and thus generate an impression of the geography of the unrest. A comprehensive 'curated' gallery of maps of the London riots is available at http://www .scoop.it/t/london-riots-maps/p/363477886/a-visualisation-of-tweets-mentioning-a-uk-postcode-and-the-londonriots-hashtag, in many cases these link to live versions of these maps that use a variety of data sources in creative ways.

I have written elsewhere of the presence of a sociological imagination in popular culture (Beer and Burrows, 2010b). With these visualisations we have something of a material instantiation of this interest in generating insights into the everyday, the mundane, the lifecourse, organisations, consumption, crime (see the official interactive UK crime maps for example), social change and the like. It is interesting that it is in the visual potential of web cultures that this is finding a discernible outlet. There is a culture of visualisation unravelling that will no doubt have a history; we cannot imagine that this is an entirely new impulse. These developments in data availability and software applications have apparently enabled this impulse to flourish, as have the possibilities for sharing interesting visualisations across networks. What this has created is a wealth of visualisations of culture that are passing through the mediascape, a number of which are sociologically and spatially orientated in their content.

As I have briefly outlined here, an emergent *culture of visualisation* can be observed that is generating a vast and mobile archive of visualisations. We may wish to ask how social scientists might engage with these visualisations and the various individuals and groups involved in creating them? We might also consider how tapping into such visualisations might not only have analytical benefits but, given their broader popularity and the latent interest in visuals, might also afford new forms of communication with those outside of our disciplines and even outside of the academy. As Savage (2009b) suggested, this may not require us to create 'whizzy visuals', although this is increasingly possible through various freely available and simple web applications, instead it might be to engage critically with some of the visuals that are already a prominent part of contemporary web cultures. This would be to offer our own retelling of the stories that these visuals appear to tell.

As well as the new insights offered by these many and emergent visualisations, we should also factor in the opportunities that visualisations create for fostering communication. Making visible our points is likely to draw in a wider audience, to facilitate genuine cross-disciplinary interaction and to append additional dimensions to our messages (see Savage, 2009b). The broad appeal of visual statements can be found in the way that these visualisations circulate through social networks as individuals share the things they find to be interesting or unusual. There is something convincing about visuals, however it is that they have been created, as such a critical and balanced commentary on their content is likely to be of increasing importance. This is particularly the case as these visualisations come to be increasingly powerful social actors that shape perceptions of space, place and culture. The representations they provide might well become social facts in themselves; as such there is a pressing need for a critical response to such visualisations, especially where they gain popularity within and across web cultures.

Clearly we need to gain a greater understanding of the culture of visualisation that underpins these visuals. We need to ask who is involved, what they are doing, how they are doing it and why. There are a wide variety of actors involved in shaping this culture of visualisation, some of these already work in universities but tend not to be located in social science departments, others work as freelancers or as interns, others are lay users who play with the data using available web-based applications. As well as exploring the visualisations we might also look to enter into dialogue and maybe even collaboration with these various actors. We need to ask what data they are using, how these data have been formed, how they circulate through culture, what software is used in the analysis, what code or algorithms shape the data and the visualisation and so on. In other words, if we are to attempt to engage with the types of visualisations that are being created and circulated, then we should at least work backwards and try to understand the significant social movement of which they are a product. Once we understand this cultural movement better it will allow us to be more discerning in our appreciation of its visual products. Prominent sociologists have, of course, already been debating what these new forms of digital data might mean for the social sciences (Abbott, 2000; Savage and Burrows, 2007). In response, there is undoubtedly a burgeoning interest in the opportunities and challenges that are presented by new forms of digital data. Despite this interest, there has so far been little attention given to the growing activity around these new data forms as they fold back into cultural activities and play. Andrew Abbott (2000) has argued that the key problem will be finding *patterns* within these new monumental digital by-product data sets. My suggestion is that we might learn from looking at the patterns that those within the culture of visualisation are making visible through their routine play and engagement with such digital data. This, at least, requires us to treat these visuals seriously as they come to envision the social world.

Conclusion: Fun and the circulations of value

As I have shown here, there has already been quite a bit of reflection upon the creation of data as a form of value-generating labour, but little attention has been given to the value created by the circulations and re-appropriation of this data. The 'social factory' is not just a space of content creation, it is also a space in which data is re-incorporated into practice in various ways. Contemporary capitalism, like contemporary culture, is not just based on the generation of data forms but on the recursivity of this data. Much of the generation and play with data occurs within popular culture as a form of entertainment or simply as part of everyday cultural consumption and communication. At the most extreme end of data play we have those who play with the data to create insights and visualisations. These visualisations then circulate through culture as they are tagged, shared and re-blogged or re-tweeted. We might also see people visualising themselves and their own networks of friends or taste communities. This is often an active form of data incorporation into everyday cultural practices that demonstrates that an understanding of culture, and particularly popular culture, now needs to be aware of how data itself has become a part of such practices and fun. I have focused predominantly in this chapter upon the visual aspects of data play, this is not the limit of data play however. To take one example, www.thelisteningmachine.org is an art project that converts the posts of 500 Twitter profiles into music. The software analyses sentiment, rhythm and topic and converts these into sounds. In this instance data play takes on a sonic property as the by-product data from Twitter postings is converted into music rather than into some sort of visual. This gives a sense of the scope of such data play and the creativity of these practices as they afford the production of vast swathes of lyrical content, that then orbits around routine engagements with popular culture and feeds off the by-product data that is being generated.

The data generated as a by-product of everyday cultural engagement do not disappear into the ether. In some instances these data get used up again and again in the practices of data play that are emerging as the mediascape continues to change, and as new software tools and the new data come to be part of the cultural experience. As things stand, such practices of data play, which, as I have shown, switch around quite and the: range from the quite passive use of charts and trending through to very sophisticated forms of data journalism or artistic visual practice, need to be thought through in order for a more developed understanding of culture to emerge. These are practices that were not possible until new forms of media, software and digital data converged. We see here how the circulation of data in popular culture is part of the fun. This chapter speaks directly to Nigel Thrifts (2005: 1) observation that 'capitalism is not just hard graft. It is also fun. People get stuff from it – and not just more commodities. Capitalism has a kind of crazy vitality . . . It gets involved in all kinds of extravagant symbioses.' I have tried to give a sense here of this fun and vitality and of how it is embodied in what might be thought of as the various forms of data play that are now prominent in popular culture. I have argued that one of the products of data play is an emergent culture of visualisation.

The suggestion is that the nature of culture and its forms have shifted somewhat. I have suggested, based on the literature, that we might use the notions of 'co-creative labour' and the 'social factory' to observe such changes, but that we also need to think more clearly about how we might engage with the emergent culture of visualisation. Where, for example, do the social sciences stand when visual accounts of the social and cultural world so densely populate media content? This generates two further questions that we might wish to consider. The first concerns the ways that social scientists might learn from or borrow from this culture of visualisation, so as to then explore new forms of communication and visual engagement. The second, more crucially, concerns the way we might respond critically to the vision of the social world that is being routinely created and consumed through such visualisations. These questions matter, but so too does the important task of observing and describing what is going on in these forms of data play and how they have implications for what culture is, how it is formed and how it is understood. My suggestion here is that we start with those playing in the social factory so as to open-up new analytical avenues, which might include the emergent culture of visualisation.

What is clear is that these developments are being made possible by the circulation of data and, in particular, by the circulation of data about culture. Popular culture is now more visible due to the circulation of the data generated by its consumption, this data then feeds back into how it is understand and consumed. These forms of data play enable the feedback loops, as John Urry (2003) has put it, of culture to emerge. These cultural feedback loops are actually now central in the consumption of music, games, visual materials and the like. This chapter argues that we need to take these various forms of data play seriously as they are now at the centre of the relations, communication and dissemination of popular culture. They are shaping how people find culture, how they view it and how they communicate these thoughts to other individuals. The pressing problem is how to understand such circulations. The message of this chapter though is not just that data play is becoming increasingly prominent in popular culture, it is also that whilst capitalism is now known for generating value out of data it is also now becoming increasingly likely to seek to generate revenue out of data play; as people compare themselves with others, as they seek to visualise their networks, as they share such visuals, as new data playgrounds populate these popular sites, and as the new data converge with new software to create opportunities to play and circulate data for fun.

6
Bodies and Interfaces: The Corporeal Circulations of Popular Culture

> Whatever the reason, listening to music directly fed into the
> ears creates the illusion of enlarging our own physical scope
>
> (Arkette, 2004: 164)

Introduction: Putting bodies into digital culture

This chapter had very inauspicious beginnings, namely the 2006 UK Snooker Championships held at the Barbican Centre in York. On arriving at the venue I was offered a small earphone for £5. This earphone fitted over one ear and enabled the wearer to 'tune in' to the TV commentary live in the auditorium. My observation was a simple. Being able to listen to the commentary via this wireless media device altered the sporting event. When people clapped, laughed, made comments, reacted to shots, when they knew the frame was over and how they responded to the players, were all now being mediated in a way that was not previously possible. When I was reflecting upon the content of this book I thought back to this quite basic experience in which information about the event, in the form of audio commentary, fed back into the event itself. Here I could see bodily responses occurring as a result of the flow of feedback. This is a quite simple example, yet it is one that shows how integrated the circulations of popular culture are in ordinary everyday cultural consumption. It is also helpful in thinking through some of the ways in which the body is implicated in the folding of data into culture.

Chris Shilling (2005: 1) has argued that despite a range of advances 'clear portraits of the body's status, generative capacities, and receptivity to structural forces, remain frustratingly elusive within most accounts of contemporary society'. So despite the body forming a central analytical and conceptual focal point that has increasing purchase across the social sciences, which includes a range of important texts (see for example Nettleton and Watson, 1998) and even an influential dedicated journal in *Body & Society*, this chapter begins with Shilling's critical observation concerning the lack of sustained engagement with the body in much social scientific work. With the exception of some important work, some of which I will discuss in this chapter, this absence of bodily analysis is most certainly true of work in the areas of popular culture and new media. Where there were some early concerns in web cultures with embodiment (Hardey, 2002), or in other cases with the more general technological blurring of bodies with machines (Featherstone and Burrows, 1995), contemporary cultural analysis tends to lack a corporeal dimension. This is perhaps surprising given how devices of various types have become so integrated into everyday bodily practices, and as mobile smart phones, iPods, tablets and the like adorn bodies in ever more ubiquitous ways (Beer, 2012a). Given this context we might wonder why it is that the body has been largely bracketed out of the analysis of new media and contemporary popular culture.

In considering the body in its conjunctions with mobile devices and digital data, we have two forms of mobility to consider. First we have the mobility of the data. To give an example, we have the mobility of digitally compressed music files as they move around networks and as they are stored on or streamed through mobile devices. Second, we then have the corporeal mobility, the actual moving bodies, listening as they walk, consuming the mobile data in mobile patterns. If we take something like mobile music, which is an area that this chapter refers back to on a number of occasions, we have the mobility of the body as it interfaces with mobile digital data. What has yet to be explored is what this means for bodily experience and how we might conceptualise these imbricated mobilities. This is not the 'dream of transcendence' to which Graham (2004b) has referred, it is, as he puts it, the 'remediation of everyday life' that occurs as mobile data networks are enacted through mobile bodies (this is also where strands of the mobilities paradigm converge, see Urry, 2007).

The general aim of this chapter is relatively straightforward; it aims to make a contribution towards putting bodies back into what is often referred to as digital culture. The chapter attempts to place the body into the media infrastructures and data flows discussed in previous chapters; this is to make the body a part of these cultural assemblages (see Chapter 2). The chapter suggests that an engagement with the interweaving of bodies, spaces, digital data, software and devices is needed. Of course, it cannot possibly cover all of the possibilities for undertaking such a task, so instead this chapter focuses upon the way that interfaces or mobile devices implicate the body. In order to do this, the chapter takes bodily territory as its focal point and attempts to understand how mobile devices and cultural consumption play a part in the formation and drawing of bodily territories within everyday spaces. These are taken as being the moments in which material cultural experiences become bodily 'instantiations' (Hayles, 1999) of information. The chapter draws upon a range of resources. It begins with some reflections upon existing accounts of the relations between the body and technology; this section moves towards the need for an analysis of bodies and mobile devices. The chapter then looks at the issue of territory. Introducing work from political geography and urban studies, this section raises some central issues around territory and begins to question how these might be adapted for a focus upon the scale of bodily territory. After establishing this background, the analysis then moves to a particular vision of bodily territory, *the bubble*. In developing this notion of bodily territories further, it is noted that beyond this visual metaphor there is little understanding of how these mediated territories can be understood. The chapter brings together this foundational work on territory with the literature on affect and affect theory, with the aim of conceptualising these mobile mediated spaces as *affective bodily territories*. The chapter concludes with some reflections on the limits and possibilities of this vision of the body in digital culture.

The body and/in technology

Clearly we are not short of research on the body. And indeed, if we were wishing to think more broadly about data and the body we would perhaps turn to work on genetics and the coding of bodily parts. But let us narrow the discussion a little from the outset, body studies is now becoming something far too broad to analyse in a few short paragraphs (for an overview see Blackman, 2008). Instead let us briefly consider the discussion of the intersections between bodies and technology. We can begin by returning to Shilling's overview of the range of interests that have driven the growth and establishment of body studies over recent years. Shilling (2005: 3–5) identifies five such sets of interests. First, he notes that the analysis of consumer culture has driven an interest in the way that bodies are consumed. Second, was a concern with bodies in what he describes as '"second wave" feminism'. Third, was the literature inspired by Foucault, on governmentality and bodily control. Fourth, of which more in a moment, was the concern with understanding technological developments and their implications for bodily reality. And finally, fifth, were those with an interest in grounding conceptual ideas through the body as a focal point; this was to use the body as a kind of 'conceptual resource'. Shilling (2005: 5) summarises these competing interests as follows:

> These five strands of social thought/analytical concerns have done much to stimulate and maintain the rise of interest in the body since the 1980s, but they approached and defined the subject in very different ways. The body was a surface phenomenon which had become a malleable marker of commercial value subject to the vagaries of fashion for theorists of consumer culture. It was a sexed object that had been used as a means of justifying women's subordination for feminists. It was an object that had been rendered passive by changing modes of control for Foucauldian analysts of governmentality. The body was changed into an uncertain and even rapidly disappearing remnant of pre-technological culture for those interested in the meeting of meat and machines which had occurred with the development of cyborgs. Finally, it became a positive conceptual category for those concerned with addressing theoretical problems in their own discipline.

Our interests in this chapter focus on the fourth of these sets of interests but reach out across a number of these other concerns, particularly around consumer culture and bodily governance. Shilling here points to what was once a powerful image that dominated technological understandings of the body, the cyborg. This type of conceptual vision reached something of a zenith in the 1990s, and it is interesting that as the concept has fallen out of fashion so too the interest in the technologically implicated body has slipped away somewhat.

Shilling (2005: 4) notes that this technological interest in the body was concerned with how technological advances 'contributed to a growing uncertainty about the "reality" of the body'. Shilling (2005: 4) suggests that '[a]dvances in transplant surgery, *in vitro* fertilization and genetic engineering increased control over bodies, but instituted a weakening of the boundaries between bodies and machines that prompted some to reconceptualize humans as cyborgs'. We know of course that Donna Haraway (1991) and her famous cyborg manifesto are the main source of such reconceptualisations. It is not really appropriate to rehearse Haraway's arguments again here; this has been performed in great detail elsewhere. But it is useful to revisit this basic concept of bodily technology relations in order to see how it has unfolded into more recent work, and as a point of juxtaposition against which the body has been largely forgotten in the analysis of digital culture over the last few years.

There are numerous strands to Haraway's arguments, but let us focus for the moment simply on the conceptualisation of body/technology relations. The vision is of the hybridisation of human and machine, of material and virtual. The boundaries between the human and machine are, of course, at stake in these processes, as Haraway (1991: 150) argues, 'the relation between organism and machine has been a border war. The stakes in the border war have been the territories of production, reproduction and imagination.' These borders are the sites of what she refers to as 'boundary breakdowns'; the result is that the emergent bodily technological relations to which Haraway was referring, were responsible for creating 'leaky distinctions' as they transgress boundaries and unsettle dualisms. That is to say that technological developments were altering distinctions between the body and its *other*. In order to understand bodies and how they mesh into the virtual and the machinic, Haraway's suggestion is that we should turn to look at 'interfaces', 'boundary conditions' and 'boundary constraints' in order to understand the politics of what is occurring and how these technologies 'recraft' bodies. By looking at boundaries we can see the flow of information in and out of the body, to see how these boundaries themselves are contested and changed. Yet despite this concern with boundaries and the 'flows' across these boundaries, the vision of the cyborg is of a boundless body that interfaces into networks and is a node in the flows of data that were then only just beginning to be comprehended. As Haraway (1991: 163) put it: 'No objects, spaces, or bodies are sacred in themselves; any component can be interfaced with any other if the proper standard, the proper code, can be constructed for processing signals in a common language.' The body in this working has porous boundaries as a result of a range of what were at the time emerging and even imagined technological developments. This was a body that could be 'dispersed and interfaced in nearly infinite, polymorphous ways' (Haraway, 1991: 163). This is the vision of the body as a hybrid, networked and reassembled thing. What we might want to take from Haraway's position before continuing, is this importance of boundary conditions and how these are both disrupted and created by interfaces as the body, in Haraway's terminology, is 'disassembled' and 'reassembled'.

Before moving on to consider this further, it is worth turning to two further key theorists whose work on the body in technology picks up on some of these themes. The cyborg imagery persisted far beyond Haraway's initial interjection. This influence spread out in a web of untrackable lines, one of which concerns the way that the cyborg imagery folded or morphed into what became posthumanism. This is not so much, as is often understood, an account of the fleshy body being increasingly irrelevant (see Shilling, 2005: 173–174), rather it accounts for new bodily connections and networks. The development and potential use of cyborg imagery in posthumanist thinking has been beautifully tracked and told by Katherine Hayles in her book *How We Became Posthuman* (1999). Hayles' book tells these stories through the interweaving of scientific and literary accounts of bodies, it moves towards a vision of 'embodied virtuality'. Hayles (1999: 29) explains:

From this affinity emerge complex feedback loops between contemporary literature, the technologies that produce it, and the embodied readers who are produced by books and technologies. Changes in bodies as they are represented in literary texts have deep connections with changes in textual bodies as they are encoded within information media, and both types of changes stand in complex relation to changes in the construction of human bodies as they interface with information technologies. The term I use to designate this network of relations is *informatics*.

Following Donna Haraway, I take *informatics* to mean the technologies of information as well as the biological, social, linguistic,
and cultural changes that initiate, accompany, and complicate
their development.

For Hayles then we have a complex interweaving of the technological transformations of the body and its cultural depictions. Hayles'
work weaves 'back and forth between the represented worlds of
contemporary fictions, models of signification implicit in word processing, embodied experience as it is constructed by interactions with
information technologies, and the technologies themselves' (Hayles,
1999: 29). These are hard to unpick, and we have to then consider
how concepts of the body and embodiment not only attempt to
depict the contemporary body but also come to shape how it is
understood and how embodiment itself develops. There are some difficult levels of recursive action in Hayles' accounts. The implication
of this work is that we cannot simply understand bodies interfacing
with information as being something distinct or outside of cultural
imaginings of the body and embodiment. When we come to describe
bodily territories and new media (in a moment), it is important to
consider the kind of conceptual and cultural baggage that might
also shape how we understand the body and how our conceptual
imagination has become limited by the dominance of the cyborg
metaphor. Later in this chapter we work with the image of the bubble
as one such vision of bodily space told through an interweaving of
conceptual, cultural and technological imaginings.

  From these accounts Hayles argues for a highly embodied approach
towards technologies and information, and for a situated and
internecine vision of these relations in an everyday context. For
Hayles, accounts that disembody information are highly problematic. Rather, what is needed are, as Haraway also suggested, more
detailed accounts of the connections between bodies and information – it is here that information and the body come into existence.
Hayles (1999: 49) argues that:

  Information, like humanity, cannot exist apart from the embodiment that brings it into being as a material entity in the world; and
  embodiment is always instantiated, local, and specific...As we
  rush to explore the new vistas that cyberspace has made available

for colonization, let us remember the fragility of a material world that cannot be replaced.

This instantiation of information in bodily experience provides the backdrop for Hayles' accounts of posthumanism. The body here is situated in constant flows of information allied with cultural representations of what these flows mean for the body.

We might ask what this means for an understanding of the body in a highly technologised environment. Hayles book is part of an ongoing project, and she is keen to emphasise that she is not accounting for the end of the body. As Hayles (1999: 290) puts it, to 'conceptualize the human in these terms is not to imperil human survival but is precisely to enhance it, for the more we understand the flexible, adaptive structures that coordinate our environments and the metaphors that we ourselves are, the better we can fashion images of our selves that accurately reflect the complex interplays that ultimately make the entire world one system'. The benefit of this approach, for Hayles, is that we can then forge more sophisticated visions of technological embodiment that avoid the pitfalls of more limited and dualistic accounts of the body. According to Hayles (1999: 290):

> As long as the human subject is envisioned as an autonomous self with unambiguous boundaries, the human-computer interface can only be parsed as a division between the solidity of real life on one side and the illusion of virtual reality on the other, thus obscuring the far-reaching changes initiated by the development of virtual technologies... This view of the self authorizes the fear that if the boundaries are breached at all, there will be nothing to stop the self's complete dissolution. By contrast, when the human is seen as part of a distributed system, the full expression of human capability can be seen precisely to depend on the splice rather than being imperilled by it.

This is a long passage but it is crucial in understanding what it is that Hayles is arguing for. Her approach is to focus upon situated bodies and their boundaries. Clearly boundaries are important in these situated bodies as they are opened up to a changing technological environment. This, for Hayles, should not be dismissed as a dualistic approach in which the body remains a discrete entity with clear boundaries. Rather, the body is not lost, but at the same time its boundaries are placed into question by the flows of information, or 'flickering signifiers', to which it is exposed. The opening-up of the body to interfacing and information, for Hayles, does not equate to its 'dissolution' into these information flows and networks. This point does however leave us to wonder how a sense of the body is maintained, how it is bounded or what prevents its dissolution.

Thinking further on this situated and everyday account of the technologised body, it is worth finally turning to work in which this cyborg body is envisioned within space. That is to say that it is worth seeing how the cyborg concept has already been used to place bodies within the technological infrastructures of the city. William Mitchell (2003) famously adapted the cyborg imagery to develop an understanding of bodies in networked spaces. Mitchell offers the image of 'Me ++' as a way of capturing these kinds of connections between bodies and wider networks. 'I', Mitchell (2003: 7) opens, 'consist of a biological core surrounded by extended, constructed systems of boundaries and networks'. These networks and boundaries are increasingly complex, but so to is the biological core around which they form. Again Mitchell (2003: 8) adds, 'I surround myself with successive artificial skins that continually vary in number and character according to my changing needs and circumstances.' But these skins, like Haraway's, are 'enclosures' that are 'leaky'. These then are not solid boundaries but are permeable and sometimes open. One issue we might want to raise with Mitchell concerns the amount of control that we have over such bodily boundaries. This forms something of a tension in Mitchell's work, as we see the competing vision of networking and boundary control at the centre of the 'cyborg self' in the 'networked city'. Mitchell turns early on in the book to talk about interiors and exteriors. On the control of bodily boundaries he argues that to:

> create and maintain differences between the interiors and exteriors of enclosures – and there is no point to boundaries and enclosures if there are no differences – I seek to control these networked flows. So the crossing points are sites where I can survey what's coming and going, make access decisions, filter out what I don't want to admit or release, express desire, exercise power, and define otherness.
>
> (Mitchell, 2003: 9)

Unlike Hayles, whose bodily boundaries are formed not just in technological flows but also in cultural representations, Mitchell here depicts a bodily boundary created by technological management and a knowing agent.

As Mitchell's book unfolds we find that the depiction of bodily boundaries begins to shift towards a more integrated and less agentic vision of bodily incorporation into networked spaces, with increasing question marks placed over the body itself and over the boundaries between it and the information-dense environment. The following is perhaps the key passage from the book, it poetically outlines Mitchell's vision of the body in networked environments, and in so doing provides us with a helpful point of departure for a more detailed encounter with bodily boundaries and territory. Mitchell (2003: 19) says this:

> Now the body city metaphors have turned concrete and literal. Embedded within a vast structure of nested boundaries and ramifying networks, my muscular and skeletal, physiological, and nervous systems have been artificially augmented and expanded. My reach extends indefinitely and interacts with the similarly extended reaches of others to produce a global system of transfer, actuation, sensing, and control. My biological body meshes with the city; the city itself has become not only the domain of my networked cognitive system, but also – and crucially – the spatial and material embodiment of that system.

This then is the cyborg body networked into wider technological infrastructures. Like Hayles, the linkages become cognitive as well as physical. We are left in no doubt by this powerful passage that Mitchell's 'Me ++' is infinitely connected and augmented, and as such the boundaries of the body blend into the environment. As he added in an interview at around the same time, where the mobile phone, he puts it, was once part of the 'architecture' it is now 'part of your body' (Mitchell and Alsina, 2005). For Mitchell the miniaturisation and mobility of these devices enables them to comfortably become an integrated part of the body (more on this integration can be found along with the notion of the 'information overlay' in Mitchell, 2005).

So far the body, in the dominant prior workings, has been a cyborg interfacing into the environment in multiple ways. As these writers allude, technology might be boundary dissolving in its properties but we should not allow this to distract us from how it is also used to draw boundaries. This takes us towards the need for a more detailed thinking through of how technologies, mobile devices in particular, play a part in forming bodily territory – in bounding the space of the body or in opening it up to networks. Much of the literature we have covered to this point is about how technologies open-up the body to data flows and interfacing. In the work of Haraway, Hayles and Mitchell we have situated and detailed accounts of the interfacing of the body with information, told largely through the cyborg concept. We also have an interweaving of techno-bodily experience with cultural and even fictional depictions of social life and embodiment. These all move towards a highly situated vision of the body as it connects into networks and as it experiences flows of data. The boundaries of the body are put into question whilst also being depicted as the point at which the politics of the new media age emerge.

The problem we are left with is how bodily territories or boundaries are drawn where the body is open to such interfacing. If the body is open then how does it close down its borders or boundaries, how are these redrawn where the ambiguity of the body arises, and how are data flows managed or even enacted to redraw bodily boundaries? If we open the boundaries of the body up, and if we attempt to find the middle ground beyond the imperilled body and the discrete body, then how are the lines redrawn in everyday practices and as interfaces are deployed to maintain and facilitate flows into and through bodies? We get a sense of this absence when Mitchell says that '[s]omewhere, there is a distinction between mobile subnetworks associated with our bodies and surrounding, fixed-in-place infrastructure networks' (Mitchell, 2003: 44). The important thing to note here is that Mitchell talks of their being a distinction 'somewhere'. My contention is that on the back of this cyborg literature, and in the absence of much other engagement with technological embodiment in new media and popular cultural studies, we need to return to the boundaries that are drawn around the body and how this bodily space is managed and maintained despite *and* through mobile media. Clearly the problematising of bodies is important, but so too are the processes by which technologies, mobile devices in particular, close down and sharpen bodily borders. This issue of bodily territory comes to the surface through this previous literature, but the nature, purpose and form of bodily boundary formation is left open. It also requires revision with the explosion of new mobile devices. It is to this issue of boundaries, the closing off of the body and the formation of bodily territory to which we now move. We are forced to consider that where technologies challenge the boundaries of the body, lines are redrawn using the very technologies themselves. To consider the questions raised by this discussion, the chapter now focuses upon the specifics of mobile media, central as they are to everyday engagements with popular culture and as ubiquitous as these devices have become, as the material example used to attempt to think through bodily territory in a context of interfacing.

Territory, culture, bodies: Making bodily territory through mobile media

The limited existing work on mobile music devices already suggests, without any real development, that listening to music through such devices is about reclaiming public territory and turning it into private space. To give an example, Thibaud (2003: 329) argues that using 'a Walkman in public places is part of an urban tactic that consists of decomposing the territorial structure of the city and recomposing it through spatio-phonic behaviours. Double movement of deterritorialization and reterritorialization.' This reveals how mobile media devices are thought of as being territory-producing devices. They enable a territory to be re-worked, reclaimed or, to borrow Thibaud's sonic metaphor, recomposed. Mobile devices are seen as being devices that afford play with territory (see also Arkette, 2004). A powerful little box then, that is able to make private space within the public space of the polis (Beer, 2012a). Thibaud's claim would suggest that territory is actually being worked and reworked in the processes of reterritorialisation. The claim is that these devices are used to negotiate territory, but this is an under theorised version of territory and reterritorialisation. We can interrogate such claims about these devices by turning to literature from political geography on the topic of territory.

Joe Painter (2010: 1090), referring predominantly to political geography, has argued that 'for all the far-reaching discussion of the territorial reorganisation of the contemporary state, the decline and rise of the political saliency of territory, and the implications of territory for the exercise of power, the nature of territory itself – its being and becoming, rather than its consequences and effects – remains under-theorised and too often taken for granted'. Perhaps the same can be said for the use of territory in work on culture and mobile media devices. In mobile cultures we also have a quite under-theorised notion of territory, deteritorialisation and reterritori- alisation deployed in attempting to understand the mobile consump- tion of cultural forms through media devices. Indeed, the notion of territory associated with such devices is an unexplored but implicit presence in this work. In the background we have the dirge of the metropolis influentially described by Simmel (1971) coming together with the inescapable flows of information of the digital age, and even the cyborg body. It is imagined that this produces the need for a sense of exclusion from the oppressiveness of modernity. Marshall McLuhan observed that '*we are enveloped* by sound, it forms a seamless web around us. We can't shut out sound automatically. We simply are not equipped with earlids' (McLuhan and Fiore, 1989: 111). It is as a kind of earlid that mobile media are frequently imagined. They serve to sonically cut the senses from the inescapable sounds and noises of our environments. At least that is how they are imagined (see Beer, 2007b). We will return to this later in the chapter in discussing the use of the image of the bubble as a way of describing these boundary drawing practices. For the moment though we can pause by reflect- ing upon these as a 'primary earshell' (Thibaud, 2003: 340) that marks out sonic territory as it is used for 'shutting out sound' and the con- trol of space in which '[a]coustic enclaves can be a means of retreat' (Arkette, 2004: 164). Clearly then these devices and the practices in which they are incorporated are seen as being deeply territorial. The problem is that this is an underdeveloped version of territory and reterritorialisation.

What, if we ask like Painter is the 'being' and 'becoming' of these culturally produced territories? We might want to begin to use the work on territory within political geography so that we can both theorise these smaller-scale territorial processes whilst also situating them within various scales of territory. Political geography might seem like a strange place to turn to help us to understand how mobile culture is impacting upon the body. And indeed it is. But there are two good reasons for doing so. The first is that a key criticism of work on popular culture and media, as I have already described, is the

lack of social, political and historical context. Turning to this literature provides us with such a context. It allows us to situate this work
within some of these bigger political questions and problems. Second,
the work on territory encounters some of the same issues that we are
encountering in this discussion of the body, but it simply encounters
them on a range of different scales. This broader literature helps us
to see how territory operates, how it is mobile and contingent, how
it is shaped. Perhaps more importantly though, this work on territory has a similar concern for understanding how socio-technological
transformations implicate the drawing of boundaries.

Following Painter's (2010) observation about the under-theorised
nature of territory, he also notes that there is a recent resurgence
of interest in territory. This comes off the back of an acceptance
that territory need not be a rigid set of boundaries but may be
part of a consideration of new types of borders and boundaries in
geographical thinking. In Painter's revisions we are returned to the
question or tensions of networks and boundaries outlined earlier by
Mitchell. Painter observes that territory was usurped by the network
as a popular way of understanding how space was organised (also for
a detailed discussion of the concept of network see Gane and Beer,
2008: 15–33). Helpfully, he argues rather that territories and networks
can be thought together. As Painter (2010: 1093) explains:

> Whatever their rights and wrongs, the implicit assumption of
> almost all these discourses – academic, public and popular – is
> that territory and networks are incommensurable and compet-
> ing forms of spatial organisation, and that territory thinking and
> network thinking are mutually incompatible ... this assumption is
> mistaken and that territory can best be understood as the effect of
> networked relations ... The phenomenon that we call territory is
> not an irreducible foundation of state power, let alone the expres-
> sion of a biological imperative. It is not a transhistorical feature of
> human affairs and should not be invoked as an explanatory prin-
> ciple that itself needs no explanation: territory is not some kind
> of spatio-political first cause. Instead, territory must be interpreted
> principally as an *effect*.

According to Painter, territory is a product of networked relations.
It is not the opposite of networking, rather, for Painter, the resurgence

of interest in territory is associated with an interest in how territories are drawn within and through networks. The danger, he notes, is that the analysis ends there. His point is instead that 'these connections need to be identified quite precisely', because, he claims, it 'is important not to invoke a generalised "reciprocity", "interaction" or "dialectic" between territory and network that leaves the taken-for-granted notion of territory intact and simply adds networks on' (Painter, 2010: 1094). In looking closely and uncovering such an interrelationship between territory and networks it is likely, according to Painter, that we will gain a new perspective over territory that might challenge how it is understood or used as a concept. Painter is asking for a focus upon the significance and consequence of territory. As Painter (2010: 1094) describes, 'from this viewpoint territory is necessarily porous, historical, mutable, uneven and perishable. It is a laborious work in progress, prone to failure and permeated by tension and contradiction.' At this point we begin to see that the issues and analytical questions persist whatever scale of territory we might be focusing upon, whether it be bodily through to global. The reason for this is perhaps, if Painter's observations are correct, because whatever the scale we are working on we are still looking at how the boundaries that make territories are drawn across networks and potentially then across mobile flows of data. Again Painter (2010: 1114) points out that 'flows are coded for (or to) a territory rather than by territory'. In other words the territory is not the thing that enforces boundaries, it is rather the creating and maintenance of boundaries in the data flows that shapes territory. Hence bodily territory and even state-based territory share a common set of defining processes and problems. Territory in both cases, because of how it is being managed and maintained, is not complete but is ongoing and transient.

A question of scale? From the global to the body

We can extend this further by thinking of the processes of globalisation and territory formation. Saskia Sassen's work on the global assemblage is helpful here. Sassen, for instance, has argued that globalisation is a powerful force that is shaping national architectures and organisations. Her focus is also upon how networks are central to globalisation processes. Sassen (2006: 378) claims that a:

new spatio-temporal order – digital networks – is beginning to inscribe specific components of the national. This alters microlevel features of the spatio-temporal order of the nation state, an order constituted particularly through the bureaucratizing of time and space ... [t]he spatialities and temporalities that are produced in these various networks and domains do not simply stand outside the national. They are partly inserted in, or arise from, the national and hence evince complex imbrications of the latter.

Indeed, Sassen's concern is largely with the relations between globalisation and nation states. This though is far from suggesting that the nation state is a coherent or homogenous object. Sassen's analytical approach is to suggest that we need to develop and use the concept of 'analytical borderlands' in order to appreciate these changes and developments. This has echoes of Haraway but on a grander geographical scale. Analytical borderlands, for Sassen, enable the analysis to move beyond simple borders to see the in-between spaces. Sassen (2006: 380) describes this concept in the following terms:

The theoretical and methodological task entails detecting the social thickness and specificity of these various dimensions and intersections so as to produce a rich and textured understanding. Given the complexity and specificity within the global and the national, their overlaps and interactions may well produce a series of frontier zones where operations of power and domination, resistance and unsettlement, get enacted. We can construct each of these zones or their aggregate as an analytic borderland with its own theoretical and methodological specificity.

Again, we see the formulation of a concept intended to find the way that boundaries and territories are maintained in networked spaces. In this case though the borderlands are of nation states and regions within the forces of globalisation, rather than around the body and its immediate environment.

The problem we have here is one of scale (see Chapter 2). Sassen's work moves between multiple scales (of territory), from the global down through the national and local, but there are only a few hints in the book that we could descend in this analysis down to the level of the body. As such there are only moments where we might imagine that the analysis and arguments can be seen on a more microscopic scale. This is understandable of course; Sassen's is a book about global assemblages. We can identify two moments in Sassen's book where the body becomes a node in these global assemblages. The first is Sassen's discussion of the embedding of the digital in the non-digital. The scale shifts here at the point where the embedding of the digital is explored in the short section on the 'mediating cultures of use' (Sassen, 2006: 347–348). At this point Sassen's 'analytical borderlands' are to be found in a focus upon the 'using' and 'enacting' of technologies. We can take this as an indication that we can continue the scale of analysis of these analytical borderlands down to the level of the body, and thus see the body as a part of the global assemblage and the 'in-between zone that constructs the articulations of cyberspace and users/actors' (Sassen, 2006: 347).

The second key moment in which the body surfaces as the level of analysis in Sassen's work arrives in the discussion of 'velocity' and variable speed. In discussing the need for specificity in the analysis of analytical borderlands, Sassen emphasises the necessity to imagine variations in temporality. Here, this vision of variable velocity on the ground becomes one of variable bodily temporalities – embodied in this particular instance by bodies that are implicit in differing ways in globalisation forces. Sassen (2006: 386) describes:

> Thus it matters to detect specific interactions – analytical borderlands – where actors or entities from two putatively different spatio-temporal orders intersect precisely on the question of velocity. Coming back to the new kinds of informal economy in global cities, we can find such an interaction in the street vendor grilling food at a lunchtime on Wall Street and the hurried top-level professional for whom the street vendor provides lunch at the velocity he needs. They belong to different circuits of the economy, but they intersect precisely at that juncture of speed.

The body clearly matters here in the analysis, it also becomes the product of global and national forces working upon its presentation and speed of movement. We have the forces of neoliberal capitalism inscribed upon the temporality of the body (for more on the forces of neoliberalism inscribed onto academics' bodies see Burrows, 2012).

Clearly then we are seeing the layering of territory moving down the scalar levels to the body, if only in moments of passing.

The problem of scale persists. We have some suggestion of territory being imposed upon the level of the body in Sassen, but this is understandably only of limited scope given her focus. It is worth at this point briefly reflecting a little further on the issue of scale by turning to Neil Brenner's (2001) critical take on scale and its analytical limits. The problem, as he describes it, is that we might be 'overstretching' or 'overextending' the concept of scale.

For Brenner the issue is not so much one of operating concepts like territory on varying scales, it is rather the problem of scale itself and the limits we are working with. The problem, for Brenner, is the lack of analytical clarity around the issue of scale. Brenner outlines a growing interest in scale in geographical work. This work, Brenner remarks, takes scale as 'socially constructed', as the product of 'rescaling processes', and therefore forms an ongoing 'processual' notion of scale. The issue, Brenner explains, is not the shift from more rigid and stable visions of scale to this more transient vision, it is rather that there is a piling-up of work in the area that fails to distinguish scale from other key geographical conceptions of space. This comes with what he describes as 'methodological dangers' in the analysis of space, capitalism and scale. As he puts it, '[o]ne of the dangers...is the analytical blunting of the concept of geographical scale as it is applied, often rather indeterminately, to an expanding range of sociospatial phenomena, relations and processes' (Brenner, 2001: 592). Brenner's warning is that when confronted with the issue of scale we need to proceed with caution, be clear on how it is being used and also, importantly, be clear about the part that scale is playing in the analysis and in the understanding the phenomena under examination. The problem is one of conceptual slippage. As Brenner (2001: 592) notes in reference to the literature on scale, 'such case studies have significantly advanced our understanding of scaling processes under capitalism, they have also arguably underpinned a noticeable slippage in the literature between notions of geographical scale and other core geographical concepts, such as place, locality, territory and space'. As such his argument is that 'our theoretical grasp of geographical scale could be significantly advanced if scaling processes – the hierarchical differentiation and (re)ordering of geographical scales – are distinguished more precisely from other major dimensions of sociospatial structuration under capitalism' (Brenner, 2001: 593). Brenner's call is for conceptual clarity in a time of complex forms of 'variegated neoliberalization' (see Brenner et al., 2010). The aim would be to differentiate scale from other core conceptual terrains.

To give a sense of how Brenner's criticisms might fit into the aims of this chapter, in response to Sallie Marston, Brenner discusses the analysis of the household as a geographical scale. Brenner's issue with this is not that the household is too small a unit of analysis, it is rather that the question of scale is placed centrally in the analysis and so begins to blur into other analytical categories such as territory (which Brenner sees as being far more appropriate in understanding households). This is an important distinction: Brenner's issue of the overstretching of scale is nothing to do with how microscopic we get, it is rather that scale is doing too much analytical work when other concepts of sociospatial formations need to be used to complement it. In the case of household, what matters is not so much scale but how this scale maps on to other concepts such as territory. To navigate the dangers we can take a lead from this observation in developing the analysis of mediated bodily territory. We might imagine then that it is ok to work down through scales of territories to arrive at the body as a component part of wider capitalist, spatial and cultural forces. For Brenner, Marston's analysis of households is limited in understanding 'the changing *scalar positionality* of households in relation to other geographical scales (for instance, the body, the neighborhood, the urban, the regional, the national and so forth)' (Brenner, 2001: 596). This provides us with a helpful analytical frame of reference.

To develop this further, Brenner points to two issues in this scalar analysis. First is the need to differentiate on the grounds of scale and to see the scale upon which the analysis operates in distinction to and connection with other scales of analysis – in the case of this chapter that might be in trying to see the body as distinct whilst also being a product of the scales it is nested within. As Brenner describes this scalar positioning elsewhere in the article, scale is one dimension in the social ordering of 'social systems and relations within a hierarchical scaffolding of intertwined territorial units stretching from the global/worldwide, the supranational/triadic and the national downwards to the regional, the metropolitan, the urban, the local and the body' (Brenner, 2001: 597). There are interrelated scales then of territorial analysis that reach down to bodily territory.

And, second, Brenner points to the need to combine this type of scalar positioning of the analysis with other appropriate concepts. The point here is that we can work through scalar positions and then work from these scales to elaborate other conceptual avenues. Brenner argues that in order to:

> realize this theoretical potential ... it is crucial to distinguish what might be termed *scalar structurations* of social space – which, as indicated above, involve relations of hierarchization and rehierarchization among vertically differentiated spatial units – from other forms of sociospatial structuration, such as place-making, localization and territorialization, whose theoretical foundations are currently relatively well developed within human geography.
>
> (Brenner, 2001: 603)

Thinking of scale alone, according to Brenner, is not sufficient, we need instead to interface scale with concepts like territory so that it might be possible to avoid the conceptual blunting or slippage that Brenner raises. This, he claims, leads to more complete and differentiated accounts of spatial ordering and its recursive relations with contemporary capitalism.

What we gain from this is that understanding bodily territory should indeed be situated both within the various scales that act upon it whilst also being open and combined with a clear conceptualisation of territory and boundary drawing. These observations on the questions and issues of scale begin to open-up the analysis of mobile media and bodily territory to wider social and political phenomena and might then lead us to a more contextual vision of how such devices play into experiences of space and place.

Bodies in the 'production of space' and the 'production of territory'

Fortunately we are not alone. We need only to look at how prominent the body is in Henri Lefebvre's (1991) classic *The Production of Space*, to see that such issues might be drawn back to the scale of the body (for a further reading of Lefebvre's geography of embodiment, and an account of how this has been often overlooked see Simonsen, 2005). Lefebvre's work reveals how the body can be used as an analytical unit in understanding how space is socially constructed. In Lefebvre's book the analytical scale frequently shifts down to a bodily level, revealing its apparent centrality in the 'production of space'. Indeed, Lefebvre refers quite early on in the book to the body, this continues throughout. Lefebvre, as we know, talks of three elements of what he calls 'social space'; 'spatial practice', 'representations of space' and 'representational spaces' (see Lefebvre, 1991: 38–39). Lefebvre (1991: 40) argues that in:

> seeking to understand the three moments of social space, it may help to consider the *body*. All the more so inasmuch as the relationship to space of a 'subject' who is a member of a group or society implies his relationship to his own body and vice versa. Considered overall, social practice presupposes the use of the body.

This indicates Lefebvre's interest in the senses, affect (Lefebvre, 1991: 224), and the 'bodily lived experience'. As he points out, 'it is by means of the body that space is perceived, lived – and produced' (Lefebvre, 1991: 162). The body seems to be of particular interest to Lefebvre because it is where the natural boundaries of bodily space, the 'fleshy body' as he calls it, are redrawn through the social production of space, here nature and culture compete in drawing such demarcations. Lefebvre's geography is multiscalar yet the body appears to actually become the centre or hub of the analysis of space. As this passage indicates:

> The whole of (social) space proceeds from the body, even though it so metamorphoses the body that it may forget it altogether – even though it may separate itself so radically from the body as to kill it. The genesis of far-away order can be accounted for only on the basis of the order that is nearest to us – namely, the order of the body. Within the body itself, spatially considered, the successive levels constituted by the senses (from the sense of smell to sight, treated as different within a differentiated field) prefigure the layers of social space and their interconnections.
>
> (Lefebvre, 1991: 405)

The production of space here may begin with the body, but may be taken off by various other factors shaping space, such as representations and exposure to culture, music, networks and the like. The above also suggests that space is produced through sensory experiences. This might then hold a clue as to how bodily territory might be created through the sensory and affective experiences of mobile cultural consumption.

The issue is, of course, the changing culture and infrastructures that I have described in this book (see also Thrift and French in Thrift, 2005: 153–181). So when Lefebvre talks of music and the body in the production of space he, of course, would not have known how these two things would come together in everyday spaces as a consequence of mobile media devices like the iPod. As Brenner and Elden (2009: 374) argue, 'Lefebvre's key concepts and analyses must be pushed, challenged, updated, and rearticulated in order to be made relevant for the contemporary moment of globalized neoliberalization, hyper-financialized capital, and crisis-induced geopolitical restructuring.' Clearly here we need to consider this advice. Nonetheless, there is value in Lefbvre's work for seeing how bodies and bodily spaces are composed against the challenge of new media, networks and data flows, not least in his foregrounding of the body in the production of space and in the sensory experiences that are at the heart of such social manifestations. Lefebvre helps us to sharpen up the questions left by the cyborg literature with regard to the drawing of bodily boundaries. To illustrate this point, Lefebvre (1991: 170) asks:

Can the body, with its capacity for action, and its various energies, be said to create space? Assuredly, but not in the sense that occupation might be said to 'manufacture' spatiality; rather, there is an immediate relationship between the body and its space, between the body's deployment in space and its occupation of space. Before *producing* effects in the material realm (tools and objects), before *producing* itself by drawing nourishment from that realm, and before reproducing itself, and before *reproducing* itself by generating other bodies, each living body *is* space and *has* its space: it produces itself in space and it also produces that space.

In here we find some crucial distinctions that outline the spatial dimensions of the body. There is a difference, it is contended, between the way that the body fills space and the way it deploys or demarcates the space around it. Crucially, the body *is space* and the body *has space*, as Lefebvre puts it. Here we see the body housed within a bodily space of occupation and as a space of deployment. Lefebvre (1991: 186) talks of this at one point as a 'sphere within the immediate vicinity of the body' (which is helpful when we talk of bubbles in a moment). The body is recursive and central then in Lefebvre's production of space, the body is a part of the construction and reconstruction of social space as the organic is reconstructed by networks and boundaries (Lefebvre, 1991: 193) and as it forms into the 'spatial body' (Lefebvre, 1991: 195). The body, for Lefebvre, is spatial in as much as it operates as a 'differential field' drawing lines between bodies and non-bodies and between the body, other bodies and the occupation of the in-between spaces. As the above quote suggests, cultural layers of production, reproduction and consumption then intervene and complicate things as the environment and resources of the body alter over time and with social change. But on what scales are these spaces of deployment operating? And how do these need to be rethought in an age of mobile media and the like?

This conception of the body in the production of space is a helpful starting point for imagining how mobile devices might enact space and bodily experiences. But we are still left with the question of how these boundaries or territories are drawn around the body. For this we might turn to Neil Brenner and Stuart Elden's (2009) recent reading of Lefebvre's account of territory, especially because, as they argue, '[d]espite Lefebvre's prescient anticipation of contemporary concerns with the production of state space, the category of territory has an ambiguous status in his thinking' (Brenner and Elden, 2009: 361). With this notion that the body may be central to the production of space we can turn to Brenner and Elden's notion of the 'production of territory'. Again, we have to be careful with the issue of scale, Brenner and Elden are focusing predominantly upon the scalar level of the state, but for the purposes of helping to develop the analytical pallet of cultural analysis there is much to be gained from taking the 'production of territory' from state level to the level of the individual body. Indeed, there are hints here, because of Lefebvre's multi-scaled approach, that it is possible to think of states as composite or cumulative territories of sorts – and also leading us again to consider how these processes of demarcation occurring on a bodily scale are implicated by those occurring on a larger scale (for example as part of statecraft or nation building). Indeed, even on the level of state, nation and region, territory is now being seen as something far from fixed but as being historically, politically and contextually configured and reconfigured (for various account of the complexity of the concept of territory see the excellent work of Stuart Elden, 2007a, 2010, 2011; and for an account of territory scaled to individual liberty see Raffestin, 1984, 2012).

Brenner and Elden's focus then is upon the 'state mode of production' in Lefebvre's work. But even here the scalar dimensions to Lefebvre's work afford a drilling-down from state to individual:

> Its variegated institutional structures encompass the full range of spatial scales on which state action occurs, from the local and the regional to the national and the worldwide. At the same time, insofar as its strategies of intervention are oriented toward the reorganization of specific places, scales and territory, they are profoundly spatially selective.
>
> (Brenner and Elden, 2009: 359)

This then is territory produced at multiple scales of analysis. It is defined by contestation and ambiguity. State space they equate to territory in Lefebvre's work, which we might at first contest on the basis of Lefebvre's foregrounding of the body in his analysis. However, this would be to suggest that the body can be somehow analysed outside of the forces of the state, capitalism and other external factors in the production of space. As Brenner and Elden (2009: 364) reiterate, 'Lefebvre is suggesting that once capitalism has been consolidated as a historical-geographical system, territory comes to serve as the site, medium, and outcome of statecraft, operating in distinctive ways but nonetheless pervasively at all spatial scales.' The crucial point here is the observation that the production of territory is occurring at *all* spatial scales. Indicating that the production of territory at a bodily scale (through mobile media) might be connected, we might conclude, to this wider 'production of territory', whether it be an act of representation of state, an incorporation or resistance of state-based capitalism or be it an act of simple consumer culture. They point, for support for this, to Lefebvre's interest in 'the place-specific, scalar, and networked dimensions of the state apparatus', adding that 'he also underscores the modern state's pervasive role in shaping and reshaping places, interplace relations, interscalar hierarchies, and various sorts of networks, for instance of commerce and communication, as well as human nature relations' (Brenner and Elden, 2009: 365). In the case of mobile media devices we have these networks of commerce and communication instantiated, as Hayles (1999) suggested, and embodied in everyday life – or as Brenner and Elden (2009: 366) put it 'territory takes on a meaning through the everyday practices and lived experiences that take place within and beyond it'. Perhaps what we have then are imbricated territories occurring in these everyday spaces as larger-scale territory shapes small-scale or even bodily territories. The use of mobile media might well be interpreted as an attempt to produce a private territory within the public or state-based territory, thus potentially making it both an act of incorporation and resistance.

To develop their notion of the production of territory Brenner and Elden (2009: 365) turn to Lefebvre's well-known distinction between the 'perceived, conceived, and lived dimensions of social space'. Here, they argue, it is possible to begin to conceptualise how territory develops and is maintained – thus helping with the problem of the severely under-theorised notions of territory in the analysis of mobile media. They argue that Lefebvre's:

> schema might be brought to bear productively on the question of territory, with the dimensions of the perceived, conceived and lived giving rise to those of territorial practices; representations of territory; and territories of representation. Territorial practices would be the physical, material spaces of state territory, from the borders, fences, walls and barriers erected to mark its external limits, to the creation and maintenance of large-scale infrastructure enabling flows of people, goods, energy and information. Representations of territory would include a range of imagined senses of the body of a nation translated into political practice, including maps and charts; abstract ways of representing territory through cartography, and otherwise diagrammatically...Clearly territorial practices and representations of territory are not distinct, just as

spatial practices and representations of space are never separate for Lefebvre.

(Brenner and Elden, 2009: 365)

So, just as with Lefebvre's production of space, Brenner and Elden's spin-off concept of the production of territory may work at the level of the body and might therefore help in understanding the production of territory through media on a bodily scale. Let us use the above passage to imagine how the production of territory might then work at the scale of the body and how it might be enacted by mobile devices. In the case of mobile media, the territorial practices would be the physical interfaces adorning the body; the headphones in the ear, the wires leading down under the clothing and possibly the sound leaking out from the earphones as the music is delivered to the ear. The ear is blocked to outside sounds, whilst at the same time it is exposed to the digital flow of data in the form of audio. These then should be situated into the infrastructure of delivery; the mobile device and the digital music compression format. The device's hard drive and the software used to import the music on to the device, both of which are products of a capitalist organisation (and which are of course manufactured through outsourcing to other nation states). The distraction of the concentration of the user would also form a material barrier of sorts. These territorial practices create and project apparently sonic, social and physical barriers. The representations of territory in the case of the mobile music device would include the understandings of the tacit etiquette that comes with such devices, the perceived inconvenience of being disturbed from cultural consumption, the imagined sense of distraction and other understandings that form from the vast media coverage of such devices. These include adverts, images of the use of the technologies in editorials, on TV shows and the like. The narrative that these are devices of social escape has been a product of the marketing from the outset of headphone technology (see Beer, 2007b; Sterne, 2003: 87–88). Here then we have layers of material and representational barriers working to produce territory.

In order to ground these discussions it is worth focusing now upon a specific vision of the production of territory through mobile media. Mobile media are often imagined through the image of the bubble. Let us now look at this as a specific example that again might enable us to see mobile media and the body in this broader social and political context.

Bodies in bubbles: A vision of bodily territory

One of the most prominent ways of imagining bodily territories is through the concept of bubbles. The most influential work on mobile music technologies is that of Michael Bull. He evokes exactly this kind of terminology in his accounts of musical enclaving and the management or control of everyday experiences through such devices. In his work on the tape Walkman, giving us a sense of historical development, Bull argues that mobile music devices have 'become a critical tool for users in their management of space and time, in their construction of boundaries around the self, and as the site of fantasy and memory' (Bull, 2000: 2). Later in the same book he concludes that 'personal stereo users construct large areas of their everyday life through the use of their machines' (Bull, 2000: 190). Bull has followed this up with more recent work on the iPod – which it should be added was originally launched in 2001. For Bull the Walkman was really the first genuinely mobile consumer technology; with the development of the iPod, Bull suggests that his earlier arguments and observations have expanded across the spaces of everyday life. In discussing the difference between the early tape- and CD-based mobile music systems and the more recent MP3-based or iPod type devices Bull (2007: 128) argues that:

> Whilst the personal stereo was commonly used as an 'in-between' device – from door to door – the iPod expands the possibilities of use from the playing of music through attaching it to the user's home hi-fi, plugging it into the automobile radio, and by connecting it to the computer at work, thus giving users unprecedented ability to weave the disparate threads of the day into one seamless and continuous soundtrack. In doing so, iPod use extends users' field of aspirational reorganisation to include many more segments of daily life.

These devices, for Bull, are about the management and control of everyday experience, the additional mobility and storage offered by the new digital compression-based devices simply increases these possibilities and thus enables a greater level of management and control of experience. (I have argued elsewhere that we might have a problem with this type of vision of such devices, see Beer, 2007b).

What is important here though is not how accurate Bull's empirically driven findings are, but rather it is the type of rhetoric we see used in the representation of such devices and their integration into bodily practice (we have seen that Lefebvre and Hayles have both indicated how important this is). What we find are various ways of describing these devices as the producers of bodily enclaves. As Bull puts it, 'technologies like the Apple iPod produce for their users an intoxicating mixture of music, proximity and privacy whilst on the move' (Bull, 2005: 344). And, rather grandly perhaps, these devices allow for the 'transformation of urban streets into privatised pleasure palaces' (Bull, 2005: 347). Most importantly we see the use of the image of the bubble in understanding mobile music consumption. As Bull argues, these devices enable the 'creation of a privatised auditory bubble' (Bull, 2005: 344). The bubble then becomes a way of imagining bodily territory, a position that resonates with the other literature discussed above (see Thibaud, 2003; Arkette, 2004; Beer, 2007b). In his later book Bull continues:

> In iPod culture we have overpowering resources to construct urban spaces to our liking as we move through them, enclosed in our pleasurable and privatised sound bubbles. Today, such an ethnography of solitude must be one of technologically mediated solitude – we are increasingly alone together.
>
> (Bull, 2007: 5)

These devices then, according to Bull, facilitate a social shield that is generated through the consumption of digital culture on the move. A kind of social, cultural and sonic bubble casing around the individual enables them to control and manage this immediate and segregated media environment. These devices are depicted as affording a kind of connected technologically mediated solitude.

In these accounts the bubble clearly becomes a way of imagining the production of a kind of bodily territory. We have two things to consider here. First, as discussed, Bull and others leave this vision of territory largely underdeveloped. And, second, we have little engagement here with what these wider mediated connections are that then translate into solitude. There are then two further issues that the use of the bubble metaphor, based upon this chapter's discussions, highlights for consideration. First, we are left to wonder how the bubble metaphor might work and how it might fit into other conceptions of the bubble as a form of security and withdrawal. Second, we have to consider how the walls of the bubble are being generated. They are not material but are more abstract, so what makes-up these abstract bubble casings that demarcate a kind of territory? In the remainder of this chapter we take these two issues in turn.

Before moving on to thinking about the formation and maintenance of these bubbles, we can reflect for a moment upon the first of these two issues. That is to say that we can reflect upon the evocation of the bubble as a vision of social escape, retreat or withdrawal. This is to situate mobile music device usage into broader political themes of social withdrawal and retreat. Perhaps the most influential and most obvious point of reference for this is Peter Sloterdijk's (2011) recently translated book *Bubbles: Spheres I* (the first part of his spheres trilogy). Sloterdijk's text is a far reaching account of bubbles and spheres in the cultural imagination (Couture, 2009). It draws upon art, literature, religious, scientific and historical texts to tell of the part played by small spheres from the womb onwards. This makes for a sometimes difficult and frustrating read (Elden, 2012: 2), but there is some value in exploring how the bubble metaphor, in the case of mobile media, might fit into Sloterdijk's discussion of the importance of bubbles in contemporary theorising. In a key passage from the book Sloterdijk (2011: 25) says this:

> Industrial-scale civilization, the welfare state, the world market and the media sphere: all these large-scale projects aim, in a shelless time, for an imitation of the now impossible, imaginary spheric security. Now networks and insurance policies are meant to replace the celestial domes; telecommunication has to reenact the all-encompassing. The body of humanity seeks to create a new immune constitution in an electronic medial skin.

In a time in which some of the old certainties, based upon celestial spheres and imagery, have been removed by the onset of modernity. Sloterdijk argues that we look, as a result, for the security of new types of bubbles. Tantalisingly he even argues that we look to generate a sense of security, a shell in our 'shelless times', through an 'electronic medial skin'. Unfortunately this is not a point that Sloterdijk follows up upon. Sloterdijk talks of the emergence of 'individuals who furnish their personal spaces medially' (Sloterdijk, 2011: 73), but these are not explored beyond these introductory observations. Even in the chapter on sound and the sonosphere, the talk is more of the affect of music upon experience than upon the media themselves; although it does helpfully elaborate a discussion of noise and the filtering mechanism of the ear as the senses attempt to cope with the 'invasive sonic environment' (Sloterdijk, 2011: 5010). This final point provides a helpful observation in our understanding of why such filtering technologies might now augment hearing in public spaces. The closest we get to the medial skin, which might be understandable given that the German edition of the book was published in 1998, is Sloterdijk's observation that we seek 'refuge' in media. He claims that 'in recent, times, submergence in the idiocy of one's own tape recorders has also proved an effective exile. The totalitarian effect of recording media can only be undone by media of self-insulation' (Sloterdijk, 2011: 407). The point here being that the onset of media noise and pervasiveness can only be escaped through media itself, media that is that have the affordance for 'self-insulation'. Media here then become the thing to escape with and the thing to be escaped from. A mediated bubble protecting the inhabitant from the media saturated environment.

Nevertheless, Sloterdijk's observation about the security of bubbles chimes with Bull's rhetoric. We can therefore imagine that this is part of a broader pursuit perhaps of shells in shelless times, of a sense of security, of a cutting-off and withdrawal from uncertainty and otherness. Sloterdijk talks of the augmentation of life with such shells and argues that 'all humans live constructivistically... every one of them practices the profession of the wild interior designer, continually working on their accommodation in imaginary, sonorous, semiotic, ritual and technical shells' (Sloterdijk, 2011: 84). In the shelless times of modernity, for Sloterdijk, we are engaged in manufacturing for ourselves an 'artificial surrogate sphere' (Sloterdijk, 2011: 26). Sloterdijk talks of media as the 'technical means of self-completion', this is based upon the types of promises or powers of media that we find in Bull's accounts in which the vision is of comfortable seclusion and segregation. Bull's findings, which we might imagine are the product of the respondents' exposure to cultural depictions of these interfaces, are what Sloterdijk (2011: 205) describes as 'the phantasm of an intimate sphere with a single inhabitant, namely that particular individual. This real illusion underpins all individualistic circumstances; it secures the solitary confinement of every individual within an interconnected bubble.' This then is where the practices and representation of the production of territory begin to converge and become inseparable. In other words, the way that such devices are imagined as having the promise of an individual bubble becomes a social reality. This type of vision becomes the means by which devices are incorporated into bodily practice and everyday routines.

What we have then, in Sloterdijk's conception, are masses of isolated bubbles, but this is not quite the vision he attempts to develop. Rather he sees this as a way accounting for 'progressive decentralisation' and for developing a more complete, grounded and differentiated account of globalisation. The bubble as a hub of decentralisation is part of a global 'foam' of bubbles. According to Sloterdijk (2011: 71):

> The guiding morphological principle of the polyspheric world we inhabit is no longer the orb, but rather *foam*. The structural implication of the current earth-encompassing network – with all its eversions into the virtual realm – is thus not so much a globalization as a foaming. In foam worlds, the individual bubbles are not absorbed into a single, integrative hyper-orb, as in the metaphysical conception of the world, but rather drawn together to form irregular hills.

Here we have then an account of the retreat into bubbles but imagined on a global scale, the mobile music bubble perhaps being one example of a wider need to cope with the uncertainty of shelless times and the pursuit of a sense of security. Thinking of bodies in musical bubbles is to think of space as being populated by foam. We might then position this amongst another set of literature in imagining that the use of the such mobile devices might be a part of other forms of social withdrawal, decentralised isolationism and material segregation – motivated in turn by an apparent 'ontological insecurity' (Hill, 2012).

Writing about these broader themes of social withdrawal, with a specific focus upon elites and segregation in gated communities, Atkinson and Flint (2004: 889) argue that:

> These various nodes are linked by patterns of movement which are detached from their social contexts, promoting a cognitive map of the city inhabited by like-minded individuals that generate socially homogeneous contact absent of potential threats and encounters. The dependence on, and use of, cars can be seen as an extension of gating and what we term 'bubbling' – the orchestrated management of perceived risk spaces and social contact while moving around the public realm in shielded corridors. We already know that key social groups (such as women and young men) have cognitive maps of urban spaces that affect the probability of selecting certain paths through the city based on perceptions of risk. However, when bubbling is combined with affluence, technologies of surveillance and enclosed transportation the effect is a wider withdrawal from the public sphere.

The bubbling processes described by Atkinson and Flint are, of course, a much more material form of segregation extending out from gated communities and providing a means of segregated mobility (see also Atkinson, 2006). It is not too much of a stretch to see mobile music bubbling in the same terms, that is to say as a form of bubbling that reduces the sense of risk and discomfort of in-between places. Further to this, in mobile music we have a widely practiced form of bubbling that is an integrated part of mainstream everyday life; a more widespread and routinised form of disaffiliation perhaps. This then is to begin to see the possibility that mobile music devices and their bodily presence in interfaces, may be explored and developed, via the notion of bubbles and bubbling, through this type of literature on urban segregation.

We are reminded by Atkinson and Flint that bubbles can be burst. As they put it, 'incursions into these corridors and the puncturing of attempts to create such "bubbles" are always possible and present themselves as ever-greater risks to those living in gated areas' (Atkinson and Flint, 2004: 889). The same can be said of these less material but perhaps more frequently encountered sonic bubbles, they are not the perfect zones of exclusion described by Bull, rather noise and other sensory experiences of space can intervene, so might unwanted attention and other interruptions (Beer, 2007b). This is not a perfect enclave, rather it is abstract and porous, open to disruption and the invasiveness of the surroundings. Nonetheless this might be thought of as a part of this type of withdrawal, motivated possibly by senses of 'ontological insecurity' (Hill, 2012) or a sense of Sloterdijk's shellessness. This would be to place mobile music bubbling within wider themes of withdrawal, segregation and fear. This is also, potentially, to place such sonic bubbling within frameworks of social or spatial disengagement (for an overview that draws across these different socio-technological forms of disengagement as they relate to engagement see Ellison and Burrows, 2007). There is clearly more complexity in this instance, in some ways these devices are also devices of social engagement. Despite this, it is important that these connections are at least explored so as to situate the body in these themes of withdrawal and segregation, and thus in a more nuanced notion of territory. If this mobile mediated body is to be thought of as a form of enclaving (as Arkette, Bull and others argue), then this claim needs to be contextualised across other forms and accounts of enclaving.

What this leads us to is the second problem outlined above, which concerns exactly how these mediated bubbles are generated, what they are made of, how they are maintained and the type of territory they afford. This is simply to wonder what these bubbles are made-up of.

Making mediated bodily territories affective

In the above discussion of Lefebvre there are clear hints, or perhaps stronger, that the production of space, particularly at the level of the body, is *affective*. Lefebvre brings these wider social processes down to a sensory level as he interweaves the physiological body with its representations. If we begin then with the notion that the production of space and potentially also the production of territory occur in affective ways at the scale of the body, then we might want to think about how these bubbles, these bodily territories, are produced and maintained through media. We can take a steer from Lefebvre's themes and draw upon the 'affective turn' in order to think further about how media may be used to demarcate or create boundaries in networked space. In short, when thinking of the networked body and its capability to use media to create these types of bubbles, we need to think about what *makes-up* or *constitutes* these bubbles. In this case we might think of these not as concrete boundaries encasing the body, but in the way Lefebvre (1991) talks of 'abstract space' and the 'spatial body', these might be thought of as boundaries of affect. This would be to think of mobile media use, and the bubbles image, as being the *production of affective territories* or perhaps more accurately the *affective production of territory* through media.

Nigel Thrift (2008: 182) describes a number of different streams in the theorisation of affect, he also points out some incompatibilities in the various definitions. Putting these differences to one side, Thrift (2008: 171) points out that:

> Cities can be seen as roiling maelstroms of affect. Particular affects like anger, fear happiness and joy are continually on the boil, rising here, subsiding there, and these affects continually manifest themselves in events which can take place either at a grand scale or simply as a part of continuing everyday life.

Thrift's account here is of spaces packed with affect and that everyday life is woven with affect and affective responses. But what does turning to a notion of affect reveal about how these spaces are occupied and how data becomes part of the corporeality of cultural experiences? Despite some of its more disorientating flourishes, affect theory is useful in forwarding a perspective of the social world that focuses upon the interplay of materiality with bodily and emotional responses. Clearly this is of value in attempting to understand how mobile media might intervene in such an interplay. In short, affect is useful in pushing us towards an account of mobile media that unpicks the notion of the bubble as an immaterial enclave. Thus it has something to contribute towards these curtailed conceptualisations of territory and enclaving in accounts of mobile media.

One of the foremost figures in the study of affect is Patricia Ticineto Clough. Clough has built upon the work of Brian Massumi, Michael Hardt and Gilles Deleuze to write a series of influential pieces on affect and the 'affective turn' (Clough, 2007). One of Clough's (2007: 3) central claims is that:

> the shift in thought that The Affective Turn elaborates might itself be described as marking an intensification of self-reflexivity

(processes turning back on themselves to act on themselves) in information/communication systems, including the human body; in archiving machines including all forms of media technologies and human memory; in capital flows, including the circulation of value through human labor and technology; and in biopolitical networks of disciplining, surveillance, and control... As self reflexivity becomes internal to these systems, an ongoing and readily available feature of their functioning, it is increasingly realized through feedback loops, which shoot off with varying speeds, in multiple directions, and in multiple temporalities, emerging by chance and out of control.

Here Clough is describing the contribution of her edited book, but the same can be said of the affective turn more broadly. We get a sense here of the complex interweaving of factors that is typical of this approach to affect. One of the things that makes affect hard to grasp, both conceptually and empirically, is the pursuit of a new conceptual vocabulary, approach and empiricism that can cope with this central premise. As Blackman and Venn (2010: 10) have noted, 'this paradigm of co-enactment, co-emergence and co-evolution assumes from the outset that we are dealing with thoroughly entangled processes that require a different analytical and conceptual language to examine'. The challenge is to examine such entanglement without then muddying the waters so much that the analysis is, like its subject, unfathomable.

The conceptual language of affect is, according to Blackman and Venn, a part of a broader trend and interest in conceptualising some significant and complex social changes:

A number of concepts have appeared in the social and human sciences, as well as in the natural sciences, that emphasize the fact that social and natural phenomena are complex, processual, indeterminate, relational and constantly open to effects from contiguous processes... Advances in the fields of genetics and biological sciences, mathematics, quantum physics/the physics of small particles, neurosciences, narrative analysis, media and information theory have contributed to this epistemological shift. In its wake, a common ontology linking the social and the natural, the mind and body, the cognitive and affective is beginning to appear, grounded in such concepts as assemblage, flow, turbulence, emergence, becoming, compossibility, relationality, the machinic, the inventive, the event, the virtual, temporality, autopoiesis, heterogeneity and the informational, for example.

(Blackman and Venn, 2010: 7)

If this is the case, and amongst such a set of conceptual options, what then is the value of affect, and, in the case of this book, how may it add an extra dimension to the analysis (see Featherstone, 2010)? With Blackman and Venn's observation as a repeated warning of what Neil Brenner, as we have seen, called conceptual bluntness, we need to proceed with a little caution in trying to gain some clarity about the concept of affect.

Echoing Blackman and Venn's more general observation, Michael Hardt (2007: ix) says that a 'focus on affects certainly does draw attention to the body and emotions, but … [t]he challenge of the perspective of the affects resides primarily in the synthesis it requires'. This synthesis requires an appreciation of the connections between the body and mind, emotions and the setting. As such, Hardt (2007: ix) points out, affect 'requires us, as the term suggests, to enter the realm of causality, but they offer a complex view of causality because the affects belong simultaneously to both sides of the causal relationship'. This is about the inseparability of the body or the mind from the analysis based upon complex causal connections. It is a conceptual vision of a tight recursiveness that makes causality more dynamic than can be comprehended with any certainty. The question then is what this means and how we might possibly advance an approach to bodies and interfaces that develops such a set of ideas.

The impression we have so far is that the escalation of interest in affect has come about as a result of some technological, social and cultural changes that, in turn, have some far reaching implications for the body, senses, emotions and the like. In other words, affect has always been there, but now it is being reshaped and challenged, altered and transformed in various ways, thus drawing attention to the processes of affect in transition (Clough, 2010: 224). To this end, Clough's (2010: 224) contention is that in 'pointing to what is below human perception, without human cognition or individual (un)conciousness, affect studies has introduced the infra-empirical, or what might be called an empiricism of sensation.' To study affect then is to attempt to uncover sensation, some of which is beyond human perception but is rolled into bodily and emotive responses. A somewhat difficult analytical starting point.

Elsewhere Clough (2008: 1) places this in a conceptual lineage by arguing that the turn to affect proposed a 'substantive shift in that it returned critical theory and cultural criticism to bodily matter which had been treated in terms of various constructionisms under the influence of post-structuralism and deconstruction'. She continues by suggesting that in counterpoint to this disconnected constructed body the 'turn to affect points instead to a dynamism immanent to bodily matter and matter more generally – matter's capacity for self-organization in being in-formational... may be the most provocative and enduring contribution of the affective turn' (Clough, 2008: 1). Clough's description of the affective turn is of a movement concerned with materiality in conjunction with construction, of the body as dynamic and lively rather than as a symbol or container. We are then returned to the type of work with which we began. Haraway, Hayles and Mitchell's conceptions of cyborgs all opened such a vision that echoes into Clough's (2008) discussion of what she calls the 'biomediated body'. In this discussion Clough returns the reader to the problem of bodily boundaries as they are challenged by 'biomedia' and other 'new media'. The 'body's being informational' for Clough (2008: 9) is not to say that it is somehow virtual, but it is rather to weave this informatics into the matter of the body and the spaces it occupies. It is not to create an imagined informational or virtual body in cyberpsace, it is rather to think of these together as information alters how the body is understood and how affect can be provoked. This again challenges bodily boundaries, but in Clough's working the informational bodies that are coded by genetics and networked into new media, are drawing boundaries through affective responses to these mediated stimuli. In reference to Massumi's work, Clough (2008: 5) argues, like Haraway, that a range of dualisms separated out the body and that these need to be reconnected through the biomediated body so as to see the 'dynamism of matter'. This is the body at the 'postbiological threshold' and it is important to use an affective approach, she claims, so as to see 'what the body is becoming'. As Clough (2008: 2) argues, 'the biomediated body exposes how digital technologies such as biomedia and new media, attach to and expand the informational substrate of bodily matter generally' and the 'profound technical expansion of the senses'. According to Clough (2008) then, this is to move away from the body as 'informationally closed to the environment' and to use affect to understand how it is changed and how its boundaries are reformed in and through information (for an account of the concept of information see Gane and Beer, 2008: 35–52).

As this outline might indicate, Clough's argument is that the bio-information of genetics and the portability and ubiquity of new media, are coming to intervene in affect, or in the circulation of affect. As she explains, in 'this context, the circuit from affect to emotion is attached to a circulation of images meant to stimulate desire-already-satisfied, demand-already-met, as capital extracts value from affect' (Clough, 2008: 16). Here we see capitalism at play in affect, as media are used to manipulate cultural circulations and affective responses. Similarly Nigel Thrift's argument is that affect has always been a part of the spatial experiences and the city, he says that these should always be thought of as affective spaces, but his argument goes further to suggest that what is changing is how affective responses are ordered:

> Whereas affect has always, of course, been a constant of urban experience, now affect is more and more likely to be actively engineered with the result that it is becoming something more akin to the networks of pipes and cables that are of such importance in providing the basic mechanisms and textures of urban life...a set of constantly performing relays and junctions that are laying down all manner of new emotional histories and geographies.
>
> (Thrift, 2008: 172)

Affect, according to Thrift then, has obviously always been a part of urban space, the difference now is that there are greater possibilities for 'engineering' affect. The suggestion made here is that there is an infrastructure intended to afford the management of affect in these spaces, an infrastructure that is comparable with other utility infrastructures. Similarly Clough (2007: 2) contends that affect should be theorised not just in relation to the body but also in 'relation to the technologies that are allowing us both to "see" affect and to produce affective bodily capacities beyond the body's organic-physiological constraints'. Thrift refines this argument still further, arguing that there is an:

> enormous diversity of available cues that can be worked with in the shape of the profusion of images and other signs, the wide spectrum of available technologies, and the more general archive of events. The result is that affective responses can be designed into spaces, often out of what seems like very little at all. Though affective responses can never clearly be guaranteed, the fact is that this is no longer a random process either. It is a form of landscape engineering that is gradually pulling itself into existence, producing new forms of power as it goes.
>
> (Thrift, 2008: 187)

There is a sense here that affect is something that can be manipulated, altered, manufactured and even designed. It is assumed that this is not perfect, but that nevertheless it is made increasingly possible to design affective responses through new media infrastructures, of which we would imagine mobile devices to be a prominent part – possibly even being used to redesign the intended affects that have been designed into the environment. The crucial point here is that affective responses can be 'designed into spaces' – through urban knowledges, buildings, technologies and know-how. This is a version of what James Ash (2010), referring to video game design, has referred to as the 'architectures of affect'. Thrift's conception of affective spaces is that they can be engineered and designed by the new infrastructures of the city, within which we might conceivably include new media infrastructures and mobile media. Affective responses are now implicated by, and possibly even engineered by, mobile media and what Mitchell has described as the 'information overlay' (Mitchell, 2005; Beer, 2007b).

We already know that music is affective (see again Lefebvre, 1991; De Nora, 2000; Henrique, 2011), and through mobile media this affect is transposed onto public space. This is to use mobile music devices, as Thrift put it, to design affective responses into spaces. These are 'sonic bodies' (Henrique, 2011) that build their own, rather than shared, affective territories. This happens as data, space and bodies interact in everyday experience. The difficulty of pursuing this further is that the conceptual work on affect, and its pursuit through various types of poetic accounts, have lent little by way of a set of guidelines for deploying the concept beyond its use as a sensitising instrument for observing affective processes and responses (with some exceptions, including Featherstone, 2010; Anderson, 2011; Gill and Pratt, 2008). It is perhaps here that the study of interfaces and bodies might both be enriched by the concept of affect and simultaneously might also help to advance how we might realistically develop an empiricism of affect. The point here though is that it would appear that the production of bodily territory is a product of the designing of spaces for affective responses. That is to say that where the boundaries and territory of the body are challenged by the oppressiveness or mundanity of everyday spaces and the unrelenting information and data flows that it is opened up to, mobile media are one instance in which affective responses are engineered to generate a sense of territory, to draw a private space in the public milieu. By turning to affect we might begin to see how the networked body comes to close itself off and produce a sense of territory.

Conclusion: Mobile media and the making of affective spaces

The undercurrent of this chapter is a concern with how mobile media devices, like iPods, smartphones and tablet computers, mediate bodily relations (Beer, 2010). Contemporary capitalism, embodied in mobile devices and mobile data, acts on the body in particular ways, both opening up its boundaries whilst also providing opportunities for a sense of territory to be reclaimed. It has been suggested here that mobile media are used to generate bodily senses of territory. The implicit suggestion in this is that we need to think about how these bodily territories, inspired by mobile media, fit into wider themes of social withdrawal and ontological insecurity. We have some very general notions of this process, imagined through bubbles for example, but this has not been developed conceptually, nor has it been situated within the wider literature on space, bodies, territory and otherness. In other words, we do not yet have a spatial corporeality in digital culture that is sensitive to wider social forces, power structures and political tendencies. This chapter attempted to pull together and compile a series of conceptual resources that might enable such an approach to be developed. In this chapter I have layered the concepts somewhat, but there is a sense of alternating scales that means that a range of resources are needed. There is also a suite of issues that need a set of literature capable of addressing problems at different scales, ranging from the global to the biological or emotional. Here we have moved from the questions of territory through to the bodily affects associated with the use of mobile media.

I have described here how bodily territories are opened up by a range of allied technological and cultural developments; this chapter asked how, in this context, bodily territory is redrawn as an outcome of this challenge. The focus on wider questions of territory led then to the image of the bubble as a popular way of imagining mediated bodily territory, particularly when it is enacted through mobile media. Here popular cultural consumption becomes a social shield of sorts, whilst at the same time it is seen to foster bodily territory. These mediated bodies are both 'extensive' and 'intensive' (Lash, 2010), they extend outwards through media, but they also use media to hem themselves off. The observation here is that the same technologies that place a question mark over bodily boundaries are also then used to enact new boundaries and to provide a sense of protection and limit. It is then important to think of what is happening within these bodily territories as they are drawn and redrawn through mobile devices. These are the points of contact between bodies and data, the interfaces, boundary conditions and the points of instantiation. The chapter turned to the work on affect to begin to imagine these as affective bodily territories in which emotions, senses, technology, bodily experience and culture as data come together. We can use this to imagine everyday spaces as being populated by bodies that frequently enact these affective territories through a range of mobile media (smart phones, iPods and the like).

We need to radically rethink these spaces as the mobility of data meets the mobility of bodies, and as interfaces both open-up and close-down bodily space. What we have is something close to what Peter Sloterdijk (2011) thinks of as 'foam' or 'plural spherology'. That is to say that we have everyday spaces full of bubbles that connect and disconnect. This then is a polis, a public space, made of lots of insular territories (Beer, 2012a). What does this mean then for public space or for citizenship? How are digital cultural forms flowing through the corporeality of everyday spaces and implicating social connections? It would be very easy to be pessimistic. Despite seeming to be a part of wider trends of social withdrawal we have to stop to consider that these insular bubbles are actually created through an engagement with networks. As Mitchell (2003) observed, boundaries and networks work together in these bodily processes. So we have anti-social bubbles made through social connections. It might be music, it might be music playlists, it might be texting, it might be email, the use of Twitter or Facebook, or any other communicative web use on the move; these are all deeply social. What they are illustrative of is what I have called elsewhere 'tune out' (Beer, 2007b). Tune out is the use of mobile culture via mobile media as a form of distraction rather than simply as a form of withdrawal or escape. The practice of tuning out might at once intervene in social connections with the immediate environment, whilst at the same time being a social act of mediated engagement with people, culture or entertainment. It will be difficult though to comprehend the impact of such devices unless we begin to see them through the lens of broader social and political events, trends and movements, or without us further conceptualising the way that the body is affected by its exposure to flows of data through the interfaces that are now so dominant in everyday life and bodily routines.

This chapter indicates that the 'production of space' and, more specifically, the 'production of territory' (Brenner and Elden, 2009), involves drawing often transient boundaries within complex, dynamic and interconnected networked spaces, whatever scale we might be operating upon – be it the body, the vicinity, the locality, the region, the nation or even the global. In the case of mobile media and digital culture we might explore the 'production of territory' through, to borrow a fashionable concept, affect. That is to say that the boundaries we find drawn at a bodily level through an engagement with such devices can be understood as being deeply affective. The sense of bodily territory afforded by mobile media is a product of a combination of physical, physiological, spatial, psychological and emotional responses to the media and the cultural forms that they mediate. If we use the bubble metaphor, then the walls of the bubble are being drawn through these affective responses. By turning to affect theory we might then be able to build further upon the arguments of this chapter and continue to further conceptualise the processes of territory drawing. The next step, to build upon the situating of the body in processes of territory production, is to make mediated bodily territories affective, or at least to see how a notion of affect may enable a more detailed thinking of how these cultural bubbles are formed and how media are used to both connect and disconnect (which is covered in some detail in Bull, 2007). This chapter has examined a set of issues to this end and argues strongly that we now need to go beyond references to simple notions of reter-ritorialistion in understanding mobile-mediated bodily experiences. This requires us to look at the context and conceptualisation of ter-ritory in networked spaces. The next phase will be to think through how these territories are produced and maintained on a bodily level. Whatever direction this takes it is clear that data flows and mobile media infrastructures are challenging as well as affording bodily terri-tory. Data circulations, as they network into mobile bodies, become a means by which affective territories of the body may be maintained.

7
Conclusion: The Centrality of Circulations in Popular Culture

The aim of this book was to explore the material and everyday intersections between popular culture and new media. To do this it focused upon the new media infrastructures that are at the centre of the relations, flows and organisations of popular culture. What this focus reveals is that various types of data circulations are central to the workings of contemporary popular culture. Data by-products, or 'data derivatives' (Amoore, 2011), are generated by everyday engagements with culture, these in turn fold back into culture itself. Here then these data circulations come to have some significant and inextricable constitutive affects. There is an underlying recursivity in contemporary culture. This book has moved through a series of dimensions of analysis in order to reveal how these circulations flow back through culture. Starting with broad infrastructures, the book moved through the accumulation and sorting of cultural data in archives, to their filtering and manipulation by algorithms, to their incorporation into the practices described here as data play, and then to the embodiment of data as they become embedded in bodily practice.

I'd like to use this conclusion to briefly think across these various dimensions, to build these concepts into a framework and to use the interfacing of these analytical dimensions to consider what these findings mean for the study of popular culture and new media. These closing observations then are really about culture in very general terms. These concluding thoughts are aimed at the ongoing exploration of the organisation and relations of culture as they are today. First let me briefly outline some of the key points that the book covered through these various dimensions.

We began, in Chapter 2, with an attempt to open up the possibilities for a more material approach to the understanding of the intersections between popular culture and new media. This chapter worked through from objects to infrastructures and then argued that these need to be thought of together – along with practices, bodies and data – in order to see the form that new cultural assemblages now take. Building upon this conceptual foundation, the book then began to unpick some of the central points within these cultural assemblages. The chapter on the archive and archiving, Chapter 3, showed how culture was being ordered and structured by various classification processes, some of which can be understood through the concept of the archive. In particular this chapter, through the concept of the classificatory imagination, demonstrated the powerful role of metadata in organising cultural content and thus in shaping where it is stored, who can access it and how it might be found. This chapter argued that different types of archive now populate and organise popular culture, and that we need to think about how these archives play out into power structures and social hierarchies. The following chapter, Chapter 4, expanded upon this notion of the ordering of culture by looking at the increasingly powerful role of algorithms in culture and cultural processes. Chapter 4 outlined some of the ways in which algorithms have come to sort, order and highlight culture in different ways. This chapter showed how different forms of agency now mesh together in the circulations of culture and that algorithms play a central role in shaping cultural encounters and thus in defining tastes and preferences. Following this infrastructural foundation, based on the accumulation of digital by-product data in cultural archives and the filtering and sorting of culture through algorithmic processes, the book then shifted towards the integration of these data circulations into everyday practices. Chapter 5 described the presence of what might be thought of as *data play*. The notion of data play attempts to capture the variegated ways in which people are actively re-appropriating data into their cultural practices. Here we see some of the ways that data becomes instantiated in acts of cultural engagement. Then, finally, this focus on practice was directed towards the issue of embodiment. In Chapter 6 we explored the way that the body might be placed into the analysis of these material infrastructures and how the body might be central in exploring the points of intersection between culture and new media. In the case of Chapter 6, we looked at how bodily territory might be challenged and reclaimed using data circulations and through the integration of interfaces into routine bodily practices. This chapter illustrated how the bodily dimension is crucial in a material approach towards understanding digital culture. It also showed how these broader changes to media and culture might be inscribed onto the body and bodily affects.

I do not wish to repeat the various details of these chapters, but the above provides a short overview of some of the key points that I have tried to explore in this book. Many of these chapters develop arguments specific to their substantive focus whilst at the same time they intimate a research agenda of sorts. Each topic leaves room for further exploration and begins to open up the possibility for a range of analytical dimensions, many of which tend to be left out of the study of culture. These dimensions are generally little acknowledged yet they are at the heart of the ways in which new media become a part of everyday life through the culture that they mediate. The concepts or dimensions I have worked with here are starting points for exploring and fleshing-out these often bracketed-out dimensions of cultural life.

The dimensions I explore here are by no means a definitive statement, there are other dimensions to explore and there will be more emergent infrastructural properties that we will need to remain alert to in the future. Indeed, in the introduction to this book I outlined the problems of trying to keep up with popular culture and new media. I suggested that what is needed is not necessarily a constant attempt to describe what is happening, although this is crucial, but what is also needed is an attempt to elaborate a conceptual encounter with popular culture and new media that may be reworked, applied, opened up and regenerated. These conceptual ideas will do some analytical work, but they need to be played with and applied as the circumstances change (Gane and Beer, 2008). It is hoped though that despite the rate of change in this area, that the conceptual ideas here will endure for at least a short period of time. The attempt has been to look beyond the surface of these changes and to see the basic infrastructural properties and related practices that underpin them. These, despite some inevitable and unforeseeable changes, are likely to endure for some time. In the hope that the book will retain some analytical purchase, I have also attempted to think a little ahead and to try to imagine where things might be heading. It is hoped that through this combination of a more conceptual focus, allied with the concern with the underpinning infrastructures and the trajectory of change, that this book will maintain some analytical value for the reader. If not, then I invite you to treat this as a piece of social history and to use it as a benchmark that will enable you to see the changes that have occurred since it was written.

Before closing, and in line with what I have said about the conceptual approach I have taken here, let me reflect briefly upon how the concepts I have worked with might fit together. By thinking of the concepts or dimensions together we can do two things. First, we can elaborate more clearly what this book reveals about the interlinking nature of the infrastructures that underpin the intersections between popular culture and new media. Second, we can present a kind of heuristic framework that can be used as a reference point for future analysis. In order to think these concepts or dimensions of analysis together I have compiled a table that outlines the concepts in the left column, the material focus that they lead towards in the centre column and, in the right hand column, I present the analytical issues that they open up. This can be seen as a kind of assemblage of concepts for uncovering cultural circulations.

The concept/ dimension	The analytical focus	The analytical issues
Objects and infrastructures	Material contexts The broader assemblage Thinking across connections, networks and structures Multidimensional Multi-scalar	The complexity in placing culture in its material context Unfathomability of digital connections The complexity of thinking across scales and dimensions The underlying politics of infrastructures The changing nature of the material context
Archives and archiving	Ordering Classification Categorisation The classificatory imagination Metadata Tagging	The politics of cultural ordering The sorting powers of self-organising systems The vitality of classification The shaping of metadata Control and the opening up of cultural archives

Algorithms	Software & computing	The meshing of different types of agency
	Agency	
	Formulas and equations	The power of algorithms and algorithmic prediction
	Predictive analytics	
	Filtering and directing content	The shaping of cultural encounters
	Visibility	The manipulation of visibility
	Encounters	The invisibility of cultural processes
Data play	Practice	The folding back of data into practice
	Appropriation	
	Resources and resourcefulness	The use of resources in creative expression
	Activity/passivity	The various types of play in cultural engagement
	Accessibility	
	Visuals and visualisation	The politics of visualisation
	Ownership and rights	
Bodies and interfaces	Corporeality	The embodiment of data, infrastructures and objects
	Matter and space	
	Territory	Connections between bodies and infrastructures
	Scales and dimensions	
	Embodiment	The shift from 'virtuals' to 'actuals'
	Instantiation of information	
	Mobility and connections	The making of everyday experience
	Humans and machines	From social issues to biography.

The point of thinking across the concepts or dimensions I have worked with in this book is to see how they might work together to create a more complete vision of the nature of mediated culture. It is also helpful to see what might be gained by using these concepts or analytical dimensions together. We can see that we might, for example, want to take the algorithm and the body together to see what the bodily affect of algorithmic processes might be. Or we might wish to look to see how practices of data play have an impact upon the classification processes that are occurring in cultural archives. Or we might want to place algorithmic processes into the broader infrastructural assemblage. The possibilities start to suggest themselves as we look at the different types of focus that they offer, particular when the concepts are combined to enable a constellation of issues to be thought of in connection with one another.

What is also notable from the above table is that many of the concepts we are working with require us to develop a highly interdisciplinary focus in the study of media and culture. The analytical dimensions explored here draw from computer science, human geography, urban studies, cultural studies, political geography, political philosophy, media studies, science and technology studies, body studies, informatics and so on. It would seem that in order to really think materially about contemporary culture we are going to need to think across different forms of knowledge and to attempt to incorporate these into our understandings. I have tried to start this process here, but it is only a beginning and there remains far more scope for bringing other forms of knowledge into the analysis. This is going to be difficult, as Andrew Abbott (2001) has made clear, there resides a 'chaos' within the distinctions that make up and separate out academic disciplines. But the ambition should remain, particularly as this is likely to provide fruitful ground for developing insights that extend beyond our current understanding of culture. These alternative and cross-disciplinary resources, as I have shown here, might even come to challenge our understanding of how culture works, how it becomes part of our lives and how it translates into social connections and differences (this was especially true of Chapter 4).

Let me close then by saying what I wanted to make clear through the pages of this book. The central observation of the individual chapters, and of the book as a whole, is that in order to understand culture we need to understand the circulations of data that are now central to it. Clearly we have always had a vision of culture as being in some sense circulatory (Lee & LiPuma, 2002; Nixon, 1997), so on the surface this may seem like a point that is not all that radical. The difference is the type of circulations I have described here. This is not an argument that symbols and signifiers circulate through culture, or that culture circulates through broadcast media content as it is consumed and replicated, nor is it based on the argument that culture circulates through friendship connections and taste communities. Clearly these well-established understandings of cultural circulations still pertain. But, rather, what I have described in this book is the emergence and development of data circulations and their significant role in reshaping how culture happens, how it is consumed, how it is experienced and, most importantly, how this data folds back into culture recursively. There is almost certainly more to come. It is in these recursive feedback loops that we find some important changes to the organisation and relations of popular culture, and, by implication, culture more generally. As these new media infrastructures have become embedded within everyday life so their part in mediating and remediating culture has had some transformative effects on how culture is disseminated and consumed, and then, through its circulations, in how it is made, ordered, encountered and experienced.

We have only just begun to understand the implications of these material cultural circulations and what they might mean. This is a project that needs to continue if we wish to develop a more rounded vision of culture as it is today. We need simply to get an understanding of how these circulations occur and how they constitute culture in different ways. This is not easy, beyond the sheer complexity we also have the problem of how deeply integrated they already are. Unpicking the multifarious ways in which cultural data circulates back into culture is by its nature almost impossible. This should be our ambition though, otherwise there will continue to be many hidden dimensions of culture that are not likely to be made visible by our current analytical focus, our methodological repertoire and our current vision of the ontology or *doing* of culture. These dimensions might be opened up by the analytical or conceptual framework I have attempted to elaborate in this book and which I have outlined in this conclusion. This framework stands as an attempt to think across the various dimensions of culture and to see into the material structures that underpin it. The implicit argument here, of course, is that we have a tendency to leave out these dimensions. This is not a problem in itself, all research needs its focal points. My point is though that this obscuring of certain dimensions in culture has meant that there have been some significant changes that our analytical focus has distracted us from. My hope is that the chapters of this book show how important these dimensions have become as popular culture has continued its historical interfacing with new media forms.

This book then has been an attempt to force open some of the more neglected material dimensions of culture. The points of contact, the ordering systems, the classifications, the structures, the practices and the embodiments, that sometimes get a little sidestepped in cultural research. In short, the book's aim was to think through the way that cultural circulations now shape the form, content and appropriation of culture within the context of everyday life. This book argues for a more materially orientated approach towards culture that looks at its interfaces and intersections with media, and thus attempts to render visible their instantiation in everyday routine life. Such an approach is necessarily interdisciplinary and eclectic in its scope. It points towards culture as being a part of some important infrastructural changes and recommends a widening of the resources used to see these changes. In turn culture needs to be part of the analysis of what might be thought of as the politics of everyday infrastructures. The types of material dimensions outlined through the chapters of this book are designed to speak to this broader ambition and are presented here in the hope that they will assist in revealing the politics of mediating infrastructures and, by implication, the politics of circulation, in the study of culture. My suggestion, based on the findings of this book, is that we need to understand the circulations of culture as they are instantiated in the new media infrastructures that have become such a bodily and routine part of everyday life. It is hoped that the circulations of culture that I have identified here will be useful in illuminating a range of other new cultural circulations along with their powerful underlying politics and social dynamics.

An Afterthought: On using digital by-product data in social and cultural research

As I mentioned briefly in the introductory chapter, there is a bit of a background story to this book. There has been much discussion over the last decade or so about the potential opportunities and problems for the social sciences that are posed by new forms of digital data (Abbott, 2000). The intensity of these debates has escalated in the last five or six years, with new forms of digital data and analytics being presented as both the source of a sense of crisis and its potential panacea (largely in response to observations made by Savage and Burrows, 2007). As I write this book these debates continue to rage on (see for example Adkins and Lury, 2009, 2012; boyd and Crawford, 2012). With social and cultural researchers seeking to find some way of using the vast amount of data that we now know is accumulating as a by-product of our everyday lives. Similarly researchers have been interested in what the commercial sector are doing with such data, both as a focal point for the analysis of contemporary surveillance and consumer culture, and also as a potential touch-point for the development of new forms of social scientific research (Burrows and Gane, 2006; Beer, 2012b).

The general concern has been with how the presence of new forms of digital data, coupled with its analysis by commercial organisations, might have implications for the place and relevance of academic and critical social research (again, see Savage and Burrows, 2007). Alongside this we have been wondering what we might learn from the types of data and method that are being used outside of the academy. It would take a completely different book to the one I am writing here to explore all of these problems and opportunities in anything like the detail they deserve. Indeed, it would actually take far more than one book to think through the various avenues that these issues might take us. However, I did want to add a closing addendum to this book that connected the chapters here with these debates. I thought it best to do this outside of the actual boundaries of the chapters themselves so as not to obscure the substantive points that I wanted to be the centrepiece of this particular book. But, nonetheless, some statement is needed, particularly as the discussions in this book run parallel to these debates and they actually cover some of the same cultural phenomena.

What I have tried to do here is to attempt to begin the process of thinking about these data problems from the ground up. That is to say, that what I wanted to do in this book was to sidestep the patterns of debate that have surrounded digital data. These debates have polarised a little. On one side we have the problems and intractable obstacles mounting-up, and on the other we have the dreams and promises of digital data becoming ever brighter. Most are trapped somewhere in between. What we have in the middle is not really progress, but rather a tension between these poles. Some take the weight of the problems to be a sign that we need to stick with our established methods. Others, an admittedly smaller group, take the seductive light of the analytical promises of 'big' or 'digital' data as being an irresistible attraction. But most, at least I think it is most, seem to be caught in the tension of the debates as they sit nestled between these inhibitions and promises. Given this apparent impasse, I thought that an important next step was to try to lose the bounds of this inhibition and to begin to think in more detail about the data themselves. The point was simply that in order to navigate a route forward in these debates, we first need to have a better understanding of the data. We need to understand how they form, how they accumulate, how they are ordered and, crucially, how they circulate. It was to this end that this particular book was dedicated, and it is for this reason that you find here a narrative that runs alongside these debates. It is hoped that by working towards a more nuanced understanding of the data, that the detail of their limitations might be fleshed out and at the same time we might also begin to see exactly where the analytic opportunities may exist and exactly what it is that they might ultimately reveal about the social and cultural world. Here, we need to see not just *the data* or its crystallisation into debates on the future of the social sciences, but we need to see the accumulation and circulation of specific types of digital data. This accumulation and circulation of data is in itself a substantive topic that needs careful analysis in order to reveal what value or analytical purchase these data might present.

It is hoped that this book will be read as an engagement with culture as it is today, and maybe tomorrow. Alongside this it can also be read as an intervention into these debates on the future of the social sciences, an intervention that demonstrates how we might move beyond the apparent stasis in these debates. A stasis that is revealed when we look back to the points raised over a decade ago by Andrew Abbott (2000). The point of this brief postscript is to draw attention to this alternative reading of my book and, at the same time, to make clear my argument that we need to understand the data themselves, in their many forms, so that we might then move towards a more informed engagement with the problems they present for the social sciences and, possibly, so that we might explore some of the ways that we could incorporate them into our own analytical practices.

References

Abba, T. (2012) 'Archiving Digital Narrative: Some Issues', *Convergence* 18(2): 121–125.

Abbott, A. (2000) 'Reflections on the Future of Sociology', *Contemporary Sociology* 29(2): 296–300.

Abbott, A. (2001) *The Chaos of Disciplines*. Chicago: University of Chicago Press.

Adkins, L. & Lury, C. (2009) 'What Is the Empirical?', *European Journal of Social Theory* 12(1): 5–20.

Adkins, L. & Lury, C. (eds) (2012) *Measure and Value*. Oxford: Wiley-Blackwell.

Amin, A. & Thrift, N. (2002) *Cities: Reimagining the Urban*. Cambridge: Polity.

Amoore, L. (2009a) 'Lines of Sight: On the Visualization of Unknown Futures', *Citizenship Studies* 13(1): 17–30.

Amoore, L. (2009b) 'Algorithmic War: Everyday Geographies of the War on Terror', *Antipode* 41(1): 49–69.

Amoore, L. (2011) 'Data Derivatives: On the Emergence of a Security Risk Calculus for Our Times', *Theory, Culture & Society* 28(6): 24–43.

Anderson, B. (2011) 'Population and Affective Perception: Biopolitics and Anticipatory Action in US Counterinsurgency Doctrine', *Antipode* 43(2): 205–236.

Anderson, B., Kearnes, M., McFarlane, C. & Swanton, D. (2012a) 'Materialism and the Politics of Assemblage', *Dialogues in Human Geography* 2(2): 212–215.

Anderson, B., Kearnes, M., McFarlane, C. & Swanton, D. (2012b) 'On Assemblages and Geography', *Dialogues in Human Geography* 2(2): 171–189.

Anderson, B. & McFarlane, C. (2011) 'Assemblage and Geography', *Area* 43(2): 124–127.

Appadurai, A. (2003) 'Archive and Inspiration', in Brouwer, J. & Mulder, A. (eds) *Information Is Alive*. Rotterdam: V2/NAi.

Arkette, S. (2004) 'Sounds Like City', *Theory, Culture & Society* 21(1): 159–168.

Ash, J. (2010) 'Architectures of Affect: Anticipating and Manipulating the Event in Processes of Videogame Design and Testing', *Environment and Planning D: Society and Space* 28(4): 653–671.

Atkinson, R. (2006) 'Padding the Bunker: Strategies of Middle-class Disaffiliation and Colonisation in the City', *Urban Studies* 43(4): 819–832.

Atkinson, R. & Beer, D. (2010) 'The Ivorine Tower in the City: Engaging Urban Studies after the Wire', *CITY* 14(5): 529–544.

Atkinson, R. & Flint, J. (2004) 'Fortress UK? Gated Communities, the Spatial Revolt of the Elites and the Time-Space Trajectories of Segregation', *Housing Studies* 19(6): 875–892.

Baase, S. & Van Gelder, A. (2000) *Computer Algorithms: Introduction to Design & Analysis*. Third Edition. MA: Addison Wesley.

Banks, J. & Deuze, M. (2009) 'Co-creative Labour', *International Journal of Cultural Studies* 12(5): 419–431.

Banks, J. & Humphreys, S. (2008) 'The Labour of User Co-Creators', *Convergence* 14(4): 401–418.

Bauman, Z. (2007) *Consuming Life*. Cambridge: Polity.

Becker, H. (1982) *Art Worlds*. Berkley: University of California Press.

Beer, D. (2007a) 'Thoughtful Territories: Imagining the Thinking Power of Things and Spaces', *CITY* 11(2): 229–238.

Beer, D. (2007b) 'Tune out: Music, Soundscapes and the Urban Mise-en-scène', *Information, Communication & Society* 10(6): 846–866.

Beer, D. (2008a) 'The iConic iNterface and the Veneer of Simplicity: MP3 Players and the Reconfiguration of Music Collecting and Reproduction Practices in the Digital Age', *Information, Communication & Society* 11(1): 71–88.

Beer, D. (2008b) 'Researching a Confessional Society', *International Journal of Market Research* 50(5): 619–629.

Beer, D. (2009a) 'Can You Dig It? Some Reflections on the Sociological Problems Associated with Being Uncool', *Sociology* 43(6): 1151–1162.

Beer, D. (2009b) 'Power Through the Algorithm? Participatory Web Cultures and the Technological Unconscious', *New Media & Society* 11(6): 985–1002.

Beer, D. (2010) 'Mobile Music, Coded Objects and Everyday Spaces', *Mobilities* 5(4): 469–484.

Beer, D. (2012a) 'The Comfort of Mobile Media: Uncovering Personal Attachments with Everyday Devices', *Convergence* 18(4): 361–367.

Beer, D. (2012b) 'Using Social Media Data Aggregators to do Social Research', *Sociological Research Online* 17(3): http://www.socresonline.org.uk/17/3/10.html

Beer, D. (2013) 'Genre, Boundary Drawing and the Classificatory Imagination', *Cultural Sociology*. Forthcoming.

Beer, D. & Burrows, R. (2007) 'Sociology and, of and in Web 2.0: Some Initial Considerations', *Sociological Research Online* 12(5): http://www.socresonline.org.uk/12/5/17.html

Beer, D. & Burrows, R. (2010a) 'Consumption, Prosumption and Participatory Web Cultures: An Introduction', *Journal of Consumer Culture* 10(1): 3–12.

Beer, D. & Burrows, R. (2010b) 'The Sociological Imagination as Popular Culture', in Burnett, J., Jeffers, S. & Thomas, G. (eds) *New Social Connections: Sociology's Subjects and Objects*. Basingstoke: Palgrave Macmillan, pp. 233–252.

Beer, D. & Burrows, R. (2013) 'Popular Culture, Digital Archives and the New Social Life of Data', *Theory, Culture & Society*. Forthcoming.

Benjamin, W. (1999a) *Illuminations*. London: Pimlico.

Benjamin, W. (1999b) *The Arcades Project*. Cambridge, MA: The Belknapp Press of Harvard University Press.

Bennett, T., Savage, M., Silva, E. B., Warde, A., Gayo-Cal, M. & Wright, D. (2009) *Culture, Class, Distinction*. Abingdon: Routledge.

Blackman, L. (2008) *The Body: The Key Concepts*. Oxford: Berg.

Blackman, L. & Venn, C. (2010) 'Affect', *Body & Society* 16(1): 7–28.

Blank, G. & Reisdorf, B. C. (2012) 'The Participatory Web: A User Perspective on Web 2.0', *Information, Communication & Society* 15(4): 537–554.

Bogost, I. (2012) *Alien Phenomenology, or What It's Like to Be a Thing*. Minneapolis: University of Minnesota Press.

Bottero, W. & Crossley, N. (2011) 'Worlds, Fields and Networks: Becker, Bourdieu and the Structures of Social Relations', *Cultural Sociology* 5(1): 99–119.

Bowker, G. & Star, S. L. (1999) *Sorting Things Out: Classification and Its Consequences*. Cambridge, MA: MIT Press.

boyd, d. & Crawford, K. (2012) 'Critical Questions for Big Data: Provocations for a Cultural, Technological and Scholarly Phenomenon', *Information, Communication & Society* 15(5): 662–679.

boyd, d. & Ellison, N. (2007) 'Social Network Sites: Definition, History and Scholarship', *Journal of Computer-Mediated Communication* 13(1): 210–230.

Brenner, N. (2001) 'The Limits to Scale? Methodological Reflections on Scalar Structuration', *Progress in Human Geography* 25(4): 591–614.

Brenner, N. & Elden, S. (2009) 'Henri Lefebvre on State, Space, Territory', *International Political Sociology* 3: 353–377.

Brenner, N., Madden, D. J. & Wachsmuth. (2011) 'Assemblage Urbanism and the Challenges of Critical Urban Theory', *CITY* 15(2): 225–240.

Brenner, N., Peck, J. & Theodore, N. (2010) 'Variegated Neoliberalization: Geographies, Modalities, Pathways', *Global Networks* 10(2): 182–222.

Brenner, N. & Theodore, N. (2002) 'Cities and the Geographies of "actually existing neoliberalism"', in Brenner, N. & Theodore, N. (eds) *Spaces of Neoliberalism: Urban Restructuring in North America and Western Europe*. Oxford: Blackwell, pp. 2–32.

Bucher, T. (2012) 'Want to Be on Top? Algorithmic Power and the Threat of Invisibility on Facebook', *New Media & Society*, online first DOI: 10.1177/1461444812440159.

Bull, M. (2000) *Sounding Out The City: Personal Stereos and the Management of Everyday Life*. Oxford: Berg.

Bull, M. (2005) 'No Dead Air! The iPod and the Culture of Mobile Listening', *Leisure Studies* 24(4): 343–355.

Bull, M. (2007) *Sound Moves: iPod Culture and Urban Experience*. London: Routledge.

Burrows, R. (2012) 'Living with the h-index? Metric Assemblages in the Contemporary Academy', *The Sociological Review* 60(2): 355–372.

Burrows, R. & Beer, D. (2013) 'Rethinking Space: Urban Informatics and the Sociological Imagination', in Orton-Johnson, K. & Prior, N. (eds) *Digital Sociology: Critical Perspectives*. Basingstoke: Palgrave Macmillan. Forthcoming.

Burrows, R. & Gane, N. (2006) 'Geodemographics, Software and Class', *Sociology* 40(5): 793–812.

Burrows, R. & Ellison, N. (2004) 'Sorting Places Out? Towards a Social Politics of Neighborhood Informatization', *Information, Communication & Society* 7(3): 321–336.

Cheney-Lippold, J. (2011) 'A New Algorithmic Identity: Soft Biopolitics and the Modulation of Control', *Theory, Culture & Society* 28(6): 164–181.

Clough, P. T. (2007) 'Introduction', in Clough P. T. with Halley, J. (eds) *The Affective Turn: Theorizing the Social*. Durham and London: Duke University Press.

Clough, P. T. (2008) 'The Affective Turn: Political Economy, Biomedia and Bodies', *Theory, Culture & Society* 25(1): 1–22.

Clough, P. T. (2010) 'Afterword: The Future of Affect', *Body & Society* 16(1): 222–230.

Cormen, T. H., Leiserson, C. E. & Rivest, R. L. (1990) *Introduction to Algorithms*. Cambridge, MA: The MIT Press.

Costall, A. & Dreier, O. (2006) *Doing Things with Things: The Design and Use of Everyday Objects*. Aldershot: Ashgate.

Couture, J. (2009) 'Spacing Emancipation? Or How Spherology Can Be Seen as a Therapy for Modernity', *Environment and Planning D: Society and Space* 27(1): 157–163.

Crampton, J. (2009) 'Cartography: Maps 2.0', *Progress in Human Geography* 33(1): 91–100.

Crampton, J. & Elden, S. (eds) (2007) *Space, Knowledge and Power: Foucault and Geography*. Aldershot: Ashgate.

Crandall, J. (2010) 'The Geospatialization of Calculative Operations: Tracking, Sensing and Megacities', *Theory, Culture & Society* 27(6): 68–90.

Crang, M. & Graham, S. (2007) 'Sentient Cities: Ambient Intelligence and the Politics of Urban Space', *Information, Communication & Society* 10(6): 789–817.

de Léon, D. (2006) 'The Cognitive Biographies of Things', in Costall, A. & Dreier, O. (eds) *Doing Things with Things: The Design and Use of Everyday Objects*. Aldershot: Ashgate, pp. 113–130.

DeLanda, M. (2006) *A New Philosophy of Society: Assemblage Theory and Social Complexity*. London: Continuum.

DeLanda, M. (2011) *Philosophy and Simulation: The Emergence of Synthetic Reason*. London: Continuum.

DeNora, T. (2000) *Music in Everyday Life*. Cambridge: Cambridge University Press.

Derrida, J. (1996) *Archive Fever: A Freudian Impression*. Chicago: Chicago University Press.

DiMaggio, P. (1987) 'Classification in Art', *American Sociological Review* 52(4): 440–455.

Dodge, M. & Kitchin, R. (2009) 'Software, Objects, and Home Space', *Environment and Planning A* 41(6): 1344–1365.

Edmonds, J. (2008) *How to Think About Algorithms*. Cambridge: Cambridge University Press.

Elden, S. (2007a) 'Governmentality, Calculation, Territory', *Environment and Planning D: Society and Space* 25(3): 562–580.

Elden, S. (2007b) 'Strategy, Medicine and Habitat: Foucault in 1976', in Crampton, J. & Elden, S. (eds) *Space, Knowledge and Power: Foucault and Geography*. Aldershot: Ashgate, pp. 67–82.

Elden, S. (2010) 'Land, Terrain, Territory', *Progress in Human Geography* 34(6): 799–817.

Elden, S. (2011) 'Territory Without Borders', *Harvard International Revue* 21 August 2011, http://hir.harvard.edu/territory-without-borders (accessed 9 May 2012).

Elden, S. (ed.) (2012) *Sloterdijk Now*. Cambridge: Polity.

Ellison, N. & Burrows, R. (2007) 'New Spaces of (dis)engagement? Social Politics, Urban Technologies and the Rezoning of the City', *Housing Studies* 22(3): 295–312.

Featherstone, M. (2000) 'Archiving Cultures', *British Journal of Sociology* 51(1): 168–184.

Featherstone, M. (2006) 'Archive', *Theory, Culture & Society* 23(2–3): 591–596.

Featherstone, M. (2010) 'Body, Image and Affect in Consumer Culture', *Body & Society* 16(1): 193–221.

Featherstone, M. & Burrows, R. (eds) (1995) *Cyberspace, Cyberbodies, Cyberpunk*. London: Sage.

Foucault, M. (1972) *The Archaeology of Knowledge*. London: Routledge.

Foucault, M. (2002) *The Order of Things*. London: Routledge.

Fuchs, C. (2010) 'Labor in Informational Capitalism and on the Internet', *The Information Society* 26(2): 179–196.

Fuller, M. & Goffey, A. (2012a) 'Digital Infrastructures and the Machinery of Topological Abstraction', *Theory, Culture & Society* 29(4/5): 311–333.

Fuller, M. & Goffey, A. (2012b) *Evil Media*. Cambridge, MA: The MIT Press.

Galloway, A (2011) 'Are Some Things Unrepresentable?', *Theory, Culture & Society* 28(7–8): 85–102.

Gane, N. (2005) 'Radical Posthumanism: Friedrich Kittler and the Primacy of Technology', *Theory, Culture & Society* 22(3): 25–41.

Gane, N. (2006) 'Speed-up or Slow-down? Social Theory in the Information Age', *Information, Communication & Society* 9(1): 20–38.

Gane, N. (2012a) 'Value, Measure and the Current Crises of Sociology', *The Sociological Review* 59(s2): 151–173.

Gane, N. (2012b) *Max Weber and Contemporary Capitalism*. Basingstoke: Palgrave Macmillan.

Gane, N. & Beer, D. (2008) *New Media: The Key Concepts*. Oxford: Berg.

Gane, N., Venn, C. & Hand, M. (2007) 'Ubiquitous Surveillance: Interview with Katherine Hayles', *Theory, Culture & Society* 24(7–8): 349–358.

Geiger, T., Moore, N. & Savage, M. (2010) 'The Archive in Question', *CRESC Working Paper Series*, Working Paper No. 81, April 2010.

Gill, R. & Pratt, A. (2008) 'In the Social Factory? Immaterial Labour, Precariousness and Cultural Work', *Theory, Culture & Society* 25(7–8): 1–30.

Gilloch, G. (1996) *Myth & Metropolis: Walter Benjamin and the City*. Cambridge: Polity.

Glenn, J. & Hayes, C. (2007) *Taking Things Seriously: 75 Objects with Unexpected Significance*. New York: Princeton Architectural Press.

Graham, S. (ed.) (2004a) *The Cybercities Reader*. London: Routledge.

Graham, S. (2004b) 'Introduction: From Dreams of Transcendence to the Remediation of Urban Life', in Graham, S. (ed.), *The Cybercities Reader.* London: Routledge, pp. 1–30.

Graham, S. (2004c) 'The Software-Sorted City: Rethinking the "Digital Divide"', in Graham, S. (ed.), *The Cybercities Reader*, London: Routledge, pp. 324–332.

Graham, S. (2005) 'Software-sorted Geographies', *Progress in Human Geography* 29(5): 1–19.

Graham, S. (ed.) (2010a) *Disrupted Cities: When Infrastructure Fails.* London: Routledge.

Graham, S. (2010b) *Cities Under Siege: The New Military Urbanism.* London: Verson.

Graham, S. and Marvin, S. (2001) *Splintering Urbanism: Networked Infrastructures, Technological Mobilities and the Urban Condition.* London: Routledge.

Graham, S. & Thrift, N. (2007) 'Out of Order: Understanding Repair and Maintenance', *Theory, Culture & Society* 24(3): 1–25.

Gray, J., Bounegru, L. & Chambers, L. (eds) (2012) The Data Journalism Handbook. O'Reilly Media. Available at http://datajournalismhandbook .org/ (accessed 23 May 2012).

Gregg, M. (2011) *Work's Intimacy.* Cambridge: Polity.

Haraway, D. (1991) 'A Cyborg Manifesto: Science, Technology, and Socialist-Feminism in the Late Twentieth Century', in *Simians, Cyborgs, and Women: The Reinvention of Nature*, London: Free Association Books, pp. 149–181.

Hardey, M. (2002) 'Life Beyond the Screen: Embodiment and Identity through the Internet', *The Sociological Review* 50(4): 570–585.

Hardey, M. & Burrows, R. (2008) 'New Cartographies of *Knowing* Capitalism and the Changing Jurisdictions of Empirical Sociology', in Fielding, N., Lee, R. M. & Blank, G. (eds) *Handbook of Internet and Online Research Methods.* London: Sage.

Hardt, M. (2007) 'Foreword: What Affects Are Good For' in Clough P. T. with Halley, J. (eds) *The Affective Turn: Theorizing the Social.* Durham and London: Duke University Press.

Harvey, P. (2012) 'The Topological Quality of Infrastructural Relations: An Ethnographic Approach', *Theory, Culture & Society* 29(4/5): 76–92.

Harvey, P. & Knox, H. (2012) 'The Enchantments of Infrastructure', *Mobilities*, ifirst, DOI: 10.1080/17450101.2012.718935.

Hayles, N. K. (1999) *How We Became Posthuman: Virtual Bodies in Cybernetics, Literature, and Informatics.* Chicago and London: The University of Chicago Press.

Hayles, N. K. (2006) 'Unfinished Work: From Cyborg to Cognisphere', *Theory, Culture & Society* 23(7–8): 159–166.

Hayles, N. K. (2009) 'RFID: Human Agency and Meaning in Information-Intensive Environments', *Theory, Culture & Society* 26(2–3): 47–72.

Hesmondhalgh, D. (2010) 'User-generated Content, Free Labour and the Cultural Industries', *Ephemera* 10(3/4): 267–284.

Henrique, J. (2011) *Sonic Bodies: Reggae Sound Systems, Performance Techniques, and Ways of Knowing*. New York: Continuum.

Hill, D. (2012) ' "Total Gating": Sociality and the Fortification of Networked Spaces', *Mobilities* 7(1): 115–129.

Introna, L. D. (2011) 'The Enframing of Code: Agency, Originality and the Plagiarist', *Theory, Culture & Society* 28(6): 113–141.

Kane, P. (2004) *The Play Ethic*. Basingstoke: Palgrave.

Kibby, M. (2009) 'Collect Yourself: Negotiating Personal Music Archives', *Information, Communication & Society* 12(3): 428–443.

King, W. D. (2008) *Collections of Nothing*. Chicago: The University of Chicago press.

Kinsley, S. (2012) 'Futures in the Making: Practices to Anticipate "Ubiquitous Computing" ', *Environment and Planning A* 44(7): 1554–1569.

Kitchin, R. & Dodge, M. (2011) *Code/Space: Software and Everyday Life*. Cambridge, MA: MIT Press.

Kittler, F. (1999) *Gramophone, Film, Typewriter*. Stanford: Stanford University Press.

Knox, H. & Harvey, P. (2011) 'Anticipating Harm: Regulation and Irregularity on a Road Construction Project in the Peruvian Andes', *Theory, Culture & Society* 28(6): 142–163.

Lash, S. (2002) *Critique of Information*. London: Sage.

Lash, S. (2006) 'Dialectic of Information? A Response to Taylor', *Information, Communication & Society* 9(5): 572–581.

Lash, S. (2007) 'Power after Hegemony: Cultural Studies in Mutation', *Theory, Culture & Society* 24(3): 55–78.

Lash, S. (2010) *Intensive Culture: Social Theory, Religion & Contemporary Capitalism*. London: Sage.

Lash, S. & Lury, C. (2007) *Global Culture Industry: The Mediation of Things*. Cambridge: Polity.

Latour, B. (2005) *Reassembling the Social: An Introduction to Actor-Network-Theory*. Oxford: Oxford University Press.

Law, J. (2004) *After Method*. London: Routledge.

Lee, B. & LiPuma, E. (2002) 'Cultures of Circulation: The Imaginations of Modernity', *Public Cultures* 14(1): 191–213.

Lefebvre, H. (1991) *The Production of Space*. Translated by Donald Nicholson-Smith. Oxford: Blackwell.

Lena, J. C. (2012) *Banding Together*. Princeton: Princeton University Press.

Lenglet, M. (2011) 'Conflicting Codes and Codings: How Algorithmic Trading Is Reshaping Financial Regulation', *Theory, Culture & Society* 28(6): 44–66.

Le Roux, B., Rouanet, H., Savage, M. & Warde, A. (2008) 'Class and Cultural Division in the UK', *Sociology* 42(6): 1049–1071.

Lyon, D. (2007) *Surveillance Studies: An Overview*. Cambridge: Polity.

Lyotard, J. F. (1979) *The Postmodern Condition*. Manchester: Manchester University Press.

MacCormick, J. (2012) *9 Algorithms That Changed the Future: The Ingenious Ideas That Drive Today's Computers*. Princeton: Princeton University Press.

McFarlane, C. (2011) 'Assemblage and Critical Urban Praxis: Part One', *CITY* 15(2): 204–224.

McLuhan, M. & Fiore, Q. (1989) *The Medium Is the Message*. London: Touchstone.

McKelvey, F. (2010) 'Ends and Ways: The Algorithmic Politics of Network Neutrality', *Global Media Journal* 3(1): 51–73.

Mackenzie, A. (2005) 'The Performativity of Code: Software and Cultures of Circulation', *Theory, Culture & Society* 22(1): 71–92.

Mackenzie, A. (2006) *Cutting Code: Software and Sociality*. New York: Peter Lang.

Mackenzie, A. & Vurdubakis, T. (2011) 'Codes and Codings in Crisis: Signification, Performativity and Excess', *Theory, Culture & Society* 28(6): 3–23.

Mager, A. (2012) 'Algorithmic Ideology: How Capitalist Society Shapes Search Engines', *Information, Communication & Society* 15(5): 769–787.

Manovich, L. (2001) *The Language of New Media*. Cambridge, MA: MIT Press.

Marcus, G. E. & Saka, E. (2006) 'Assemblage', *Theory, Culture & Society* 23(2–3): 101–106.

Miller, D. (2008) *The Comfort of Things*. Cambridge: Polity.

Miller, D. (2010) *Stuff*. Cambridge: Polity.

Mills, C. W. (1959) *The Sociological Imagination*. Oxford: Oxford University Press.

Mitall, P. (2012) 'Features in Multi-media Archives', Presentation at the ESRC Real-Time Research Methods event *New Questions for New Times and New Places*, University of York, 23 March 2012.

Mitchell, W. J. (2003) *Me++: The Cyborg Self and the Networked City*. Cambridge, MA: MIT Press.

Mitchell, W. J. (2005) *Placing Words: Symbols, Space, and the City*. Cambridge, MA: The MIT Press.

Mitchell, W. & Alsina, P. (2005) Interview: William J. Mitchell. ArtNodes, January 2005, http://www.uoc.edu/artnodes/espai/eng/art/pdf/mitchell1204 .pdf (accessed 8 May 2012).

Morris, J. W. (2012) 'Making Music Behave: Metadata and the Digital Music Commodity', *New Media & Society*, online first DOI: 10.1177/ 1461444811430645 (accessed 12 May 2012).

Netflix. (2012) 'Netflix Recommendations: Beyond the 5 Stars (part 1)', The Netflix Tech Blog, Friday 6 April 2012, http://techblog.netflix.com/ 2012/04/netflix-recommendations-beyond-5-stars.html (accessed 29 May 2012).

Nettleton, S. & Watson, J. (1998) *The Body in Everyday Life*. London: Routledge.

Nixon, S. (1997) 'Circulating Culture', in DuGay, P. (ed.) *Production of Culture/Cultures of Production*. London: The Open University Press, pp. 177–234.

Osborne, T. (1999) 'The Ordinariness of the Archive', *History of the Human Sciences* 12(2): 51–64.

Painter, J. (2010) 'Rethinking Territory', *Antipode* 42(5): 1090–1118.

Parikka, J. (2010) *Insect Media: An Archeology of Animals and Technology*. Minneapolis: University of Minnesota Press.

Parikka, J. (2012) *What Is Media Archaeology?* Cambridge: Polity.

Poster, M. (1995) *The Second Media Age.* Cambridge: Polity.

Raffestin, C. (1984) 'Territoriality: A Reflection of the Discrepancies between the Organization of Space and the Individual Liberty', *International Political Science Review* 5(2): 139–146.

Raffestin, C. (2012) 'Space, Territory, and Territoriality', *Environment and Planning D: Society and Space* 30(1): 121–141.

Rankin, K. N. (2011) 'Assemblage and the Politics of Thick Description', CITY 15(5): 563–568.

Ritzer, G. & Jurgensen, N. (2010) 'Production, Consumption, Prosumption: The Nature of Capitalism in the Age of the Digital "prosumer" ', *Journal of Consumer Culture* 10(1): 13–36.

Ruppert, E. (2011) 'Population Objects: Interpassive Subjects', *Sociology* 45(2): 218–233.

Ruppert, E. & Savage, M. (2012) 'Transactional Politics', *The Sociological Review* 59(s2): 73–92.

Rushe, D. (2012) 'Facebook Narrowly Avoids Dip Below Starting Price in Mixed First Day of IPO', *The Guardian*, 18 May 2012.

Sassen, S. (2006) *Territory, Authority, Rights: From Medieval to Global Assemblages.* Princeton: Princeton University Press.

Savage, S. (2009a) 'Against Epochalism: An Analysis of Conceptions of Change in British Sociology', *Cultural Sociology* 3(2): 217–238.

Savage, M. (2009b) 'Contemporary Sociology and the Challenge of Descriptive Assemblage', *European Journal of Social Theory* 12(1): 155–174.

Savage, M. & Gayo, M. (2011) 'Unravelling the Omnivore: A Field Analysis of Contemporary Musical Taste in the United Kingdom', *Poetics* 39(5): 337–357.

Savage, M. & Burrows, R. (2007) 'The Coming Crisis of Empirical Sociology', *Sociology* 41(5): 885–900.

Scholz, T. (ed.) (2012) *Digital Labor: The Internet as Playground and Factory.* London: Routledge.

Sedgewick, R. (1988) *Algorithms.* Second Edition. MA: Addison Wesley.

Shilling, C. (2005) *The Body in Culture, Technology & Society.* London: Sage.

Simmel, G. (1971) 'The Metropolis and Mental Life', in Levine, D. N. (ed) *On Individuality and Social Forms.* Chicago and London: The University of Chicago Press, pp. 324–339.

Simonsen, K. (2005) 'Bodies, Sensations, Space and Time: The Contribution from Henri Lefebvre', *Geografiska Annaler* 87 B (1): 1–14.

Sloterdijk, P. (2011) *Bubbles: Spheres I*, translated by Wieland Hoban. Los Angeles: Semiotext(e).

Spector, R. (2002) *Amazon.com: Get Big Fast.* New York: Harper Business.

Sterling, B. (2005) *Shaping Things.* Cambridge, MA: The MIT Press.

Sterne, J. (2003) *The Audible Past: Cultural Origins of Sound Reproduction.* Durham & London: Duke University Press.

Sterne, J. (2012) *MP3: The Meaning of a Format.* Durham and London: Duke University Press.

Terranova, T. (2000) 'Free Labor: Producing Culture for the Digital Economy', *Social Text* 18(2): 33–58.

Thacker, E. (2007) 'Pulse Demons', *Culture Machine* 9: http://www.culturemachine.net/index.php/cm/article/viewArticle/80/56 (accessed 28 May 2012).

Thibaud, J. P. (2003) 'The Sonic Composition of the City', in Bull, M. & Back, L. (eds) *The Auditory Culture Reader*. Oxford: Berg, pp. 329–342.

Thornton, S. (1995) *Club Cultures*. Cambridge: Polity.

Thrift, N. (2005) *Knowing Capitalism*. London: Sage.

Thrift, N. (2008) *Non-Representational Theory: Space Politics Affect*. London: Routledge.

Turkle, S. (2007) *Evocative Objects: Things We Think With*. Cambridge, MA: MIT Press.

Turow, J. (2006) *Niche Envy: Marketing Discrimination in the Digital Age*. Cambridge, MA: MIT Press.

Tomlinson, J. (2007) *The Culture of Speed: The Coming of Immediacy*. London: Sage.

Turner, G. (2010) *Ordinary People and the Media: The Demotic Turn*. London: Sage.

Uprichard, E., Burrows, R. & Byrne, D. (2009) 'SPSS as an "inscription device": From Causality to Description?', *The Sociological Review* 56(4): 606–622.

Urry, J. (2003) *Global Complexity*. Cambridge: Polity.

Urry, J. (2007) *Mobilities*. Cambridge: Polity.

Venn, C. (2006) 'A Note on Assemblage', *Theory, Culture & Society* 23(2–3): 107–108.

Wachsmuth, D., Madden, D. J. & Brenner, N. (2011) 'Between Abstraction and Complexity: Meta-theoretical Observations on the Assemblage Debate', *CITY* 15(6): 740–749.

Wilf, H. S. (2002) *Algorithms and Complexity*. Second Edition. MA: A K Peters.

Woolgar, B. (2002) *Virtual Society? Technology, Cyberbole, Reality*. Oxford: Oxford University Press.

Yau, N. (2011) *Visualize This: The Flowing Data Guide to Design, Visualization, and Statistics*. Indianapolis: Wiley.

Index

experience, 1, 4, 6, 10, 22, 28, 35, 37, 58, 61, 82, 92, 100, 120, 123–4, 128–9, 132, 141–51, 154–5, 159–64, 169, 171

Facebook, 52–4, 58, 66, 90–1, 97, 101–4, 109–10, 163
fear, 53, 129, 154–5
Featherstone, M., 9, 40, 46–53, 61, 123, 157, 161
feedback, 11, 37, 83, 92, 94, 121–2, 127, 156, 171
fiction, 18, 128, 132
film, 50, 63, 81, 92, 96, 101, 181
Flickr, 53, 109, 111
flow, 2–4, 9–12, 21, 23, 25, 31, 49, 59–60, 68, 71, 82–5, 104–5, 116, 122, 124, 126–36, 143, 146–7, 156–7, 161–5
format, 4, 15, 21, 48, 53, 61, 99
Foucault, M., 22, 43–7, 60–1, 125
free labour, 102, 104, 106–11
Fuller, M., 26–7
function, 13, 16, 20, 27, 30, 34, 60, 66–8, 73, 75–6, 79–81, 85–6, 89–90, 92, 94, 99, 156
future, 35, 61, 65, 87, 94, 112, 167–8

Galloway, A., 69, 90
Gane, N., 4–6, 18–19, 24, 28, 36, 38, 46–7, 73, 107, 135, 159, 167
genre, 44
geography, 34, 78, 117, 124, 133–4, 141–2, 170
Gill, R., 11, 22, 32, 102–3, 107, 155, 161
global, 1, 3, 21, 29–33, 53, 57, 60–1, 84–5, 131, 136–40, 143, 152, 162–3
globalisation, 31, 136–8, 152
Google, 13, 48–9, 58, 66, 89, 94, 96, 101, 110, 115
Graham, S., 19, 23–7, 51, 70, 73, 75–8, 84, 98, 107, 123
group, 4, 10, 42, 64, 84, 89, 91, 95–6, 111, 117, 142, 153

Haraway, D., 27, 126–30, 132, 137, 158
Hardey, M., 115, 123
Hardt, M., 155, 157
Harvey, P., 23, 87
Hayles, N.K., 11, 19–20, 48, 67, 70, 86, 124, 127–32, 146, 149, 158
headphone, 147
Hesmondhalgh, D., 105–8
Hill, D., 152, 154
home, 48, 73, 85, 88, 148

identification, 25, 88
identity, 18, 26, 32–3
ideology, 48, 69, 82–3, 89–90
image, 20, 25, 46, 66, 69, 75, 80, 93, 113, 116, 125–30, 134, 147, 149, 155, 159–62
imagination, 34, 41–6, 49, 53, 55–6, 60–1, 126, 128, 150, 166, 168
immaterial, 18, 105, 157
in-between, 137–8, 144, 148, 153
individual, 7, 11, 14–17, 28, 30, 36, 42, 45–8, 58–60, 64, 71, 74, 77, 83–4, 87–9, 92, 95–6, 101–2, 106, 110–11, 115–21, 144–5, 149–53, 157, 170
individualisation, 47
inescapable, 28, 43, 134
information, 10–11, 14, 18–26, 29, 38, 46, 49, 53–8, 66, 69, 75–8, 81–4, 90, 111, 114–15, 122, 126–34, 146, 156–61, 169
infrastructure, 1–31, 33, 35–41, 50, 52–5, 60–3, 75–6, 79, 82, 84, 91, 96–9, 102, 124, 130–1, 143, 146–7, 159–60, 164–72
interface, 11–13, 78, 110–11, 122–9, 131–63, 167, 169, 171
internet, 6, 26, 49, 66, 103–5
iPad, 13, 16, 20
iPhone, 16
iPod, 16, 20, 123, 143, 148–9, 161, 162
iteration/iterative, 78, 82–4

Printed and bound in Great Britain by
CPI Antony Rowe, Chippenham and Eastbourne